D0147232

Criminal Justice
Recent Scholarship

Edited by
Marilyn McShane and Frank P. Williams III

A Series from LFB Scholarly

After the Insanity Defense
When the Acquitted Return to the Community

Matthew F. Shaw

LFB Scholarly Publishing LLC
New York 2007

Library of Congress Cataloging-in-Publication Data

Shaw, Matthew F., 1972-
 After the insanity defense : when the acquitted return to the
community / Matthew F. Shaw.
    p. cm. -- (Criminal justice recent scholarship)
 Includes bibliographical references and index.
 ISBN 1-59332-147-3 (alk. paper)
 1. Mentally ill offenders. 2. Recidivism. 3. Criminal behavior,
Prediction of. 4. Mentally ill offenders--United States. 5. Recidivism--
United States. I. Title.
 HV6133.S45 2007
 364.8--dc22

2006025693

ISBN 1-59332-147-3

Printed on acid-free 250-year-life paper.

Manufactured in the United States of America.

Table of Contents

List of Tables

List of Figures

Acknowledgements

A national health services fellowship, managed by the Hines Veteran's Administration Hospital, provided sustained financial backing, invaluable collegial input, and broad institutional resources for this project. Eric Vandenburg, Ph.D., Ken Conrad, Ph.D., and Kevin Weiss, M.D. administered the fellowship and shaped the scope and structure of the research.

At the Feinberg School of Medicine at Northwestern University, Peter Zeldow, Ph.D., Thomas Simpatico, M.D., Gene Griffin, J.D., Ph.D., and John Lyons, Ph.D. offered their extensive experience working within the criminal justice and mental health systems and conducting large evaluation studies.

At Yale University, Howard Zonana, M.D. and Ernst Prelinger, Ph.D. shared their insights concerning the insanity defense. Joseph Bloom, M.D. provided useful information about practices in Oregon.

CHAPTER 1

Studying Recidivism

In rare instances, criminal offenders are not held responsible for crimes that they have committed, because they were mentally impaired at the time of the offense. They are found Not Guilty by Reason of Insanity (NGRI), because their behavior is attributable to a mental illness rather than a moral failing. In providing mental health services to these unique offenders, administrators and clinicians must continually balance two seemingly contradictory concerns. We must provide services in the least restrictive setting possible while also protecting members of the community from post-discharge criminal activity.[1] In a 1978 New Jersey insanity case, *State v. Fields*, these competing concerns were raised as follows: "The new order should provide for the least restrictive restraints which are found by the judge to be consistent with the well-being of the community and the individual." If we lock acquittees away in psychiatric facilities without proper clinical justification, we violate their fundamental rights. If we release them into the community before they have sufficient control of their cognition and behavior, we risk endangering members of the community and possibly the acquittees themselves.

The following questions are integral to finding an effective balance between these competing concerns: How risky is it for acquittees to be released into the community? How does the level of risk vary across individuals and contexts? Lastly, what outpatient treatments, monitoring

1

procedures and tracking protocols manage the risk most effectively? The following chapter is a review of the literature pertaining to criminal recidivism for insanity acquittees. It provides the backdrop for answering the preceding questions. I will discuss the broad range of recidivism rates, correlates of recidivism and interventions associated with reductions that have been identified in prior studies. In doing so, I will highlight the methodological shortcomings that limit the integration of results across studies, and propose a new research agenda. The proposal will call for the incorporation of broader clinical material and the development of a more sophisticated understanding of time as a factor. The long-term goal of implementing the proposed course of study is to identify the most effective treatment pathways, as defined both by improved clinical outcomes and reduced criminal recidivism, and in so doing, to differentiate subsets of NGRI acquittees by clinical and actuarial measures of risk. Once such pathways are identified, a tracking system can be developed to assess the effectiveness of NGRI service delivery systems. The tracking system ideally would be used to enhance clinical outcomes while reducing post-discharge criminality, thereby balancing the central concerns of administrators, clinicians, and the public.

Legislative Reforms
The insanity defense has been active in varying forms since the Middle Ages.[2] Although the criteria used to assess insanity and the efficacy of the legal strategies have varied over time, the defense itself has endured. Variations within the United States have clustered around three groups of guidelines: the M'Naughten rules; The Durham rules; and the American Law Institute (A.L.I.) rules.

In 1843, Daniel M'Naghten was accused of murdering Edward Drummond, the English Prime Minister's private secretary. Though he admitted to committing the act, he was acquitted, because he was not considered "capable of distinguishing right from wrong with respect to the act of which he [stood] charged."[3] The public decried the decision—a reaction that remains common 150 years later. British officials responded to the ensuing turmoil by formalizing the criteria used in insanity cases. The guidelines they designed, referred to as the M'Naghten Rule, addressed the cognitive capacities of the accused individual. In order for a person to be considered sane, and therefore criminally responsible, the person must be aware both of the actions committed and their immorality.[4]

In 1851, the majority of state and federal courts in the United States adopted the M'Naghten rule. During the next century, various states altered it in order to address volitional as well as cognitive criteria; however, the rule remained primarily concerned with the accused person's cognitive state. The Durham rule, established in 1954 in the District of Columbia, was the first significant and widely accepted transformation of the M'Naghten rule. Rather than addressing the impaired judgment of insane individuals, it referred to those behaviors considered "products" of mental defect or disease. Once the legal and mental health communities realized the difficulties in elucidating the term "product" and identifying causal pathways that "produce" behavior, the rule was soon disregarded.[5]

In 1962, legal experts at the American Law Institute (A.L.I) proposed the Model Penal Code. It contained criteria for the insanity defense that differed significantly from previous rules. The A.L.I. rule not only addressed the cognitive components of sanity but also explicitly addressed the volitional components. "A person is not responsible for criminal conduct if at the time of such conduct, as a result of mental disease or defect, he lacks substantial capacity either to appreciate the criminality [wrongfulness] of his conduct or to conform his conduct to the requirements of the law."[6] The added element of concern for the ability to conform one's behavior—in other words, to resist compulsions—broadened the use of the insanity defense considerably.[7]

In 1982, John Hinckley Jr. was acquitted by reason of insanity for the attempted assassination of President Reagan. There was broad public criticism of the decision, and Congress responded by passing the Insanity Defense Reform Act in 1984. This piece of legislation was the first federal code for insanity cases. It transferred the burden of proof from the prosecution to the defense, eliminated the volitional criterion of the A.L.I. standard, eliminated the diminished capacity defense, and mandated publicly supervised treatment. During the early to mid-eighties, legislators in nearly every state reformed their insanity rules.[8] Directly following the Hinkley verdict, 34 states modified segments of their extant statutes regarding NGRI acquittal.[9]

Insanity Acquittees
There are two primary concepts addressing the cognitive and behavioral capacities of persons entering the criminal justice system: the fitness standard and the insanity defense. The fitness standard, also known as competency, refers to an individual's capacity to participate in judicial actions. It addresses an offender's ability to understand the proceedings and charges, and participate in the defense as

required by the U.S. Constitution. Assessments of fitness therefore demand present-state examinations.[10] Insanity, however, is a legal term that applies to the mental state of an offender at the time of an incident. Insanity assessments therefore demand comprehensive examinations of present mental status, developmental history, psychiatric history and recent functioning.[11]

Though mental health professionals conduct insanity examinations, the courts are ultimately responsible for assessing whether an insanity defense is successful or not. A person labeled insane often must meet the criteria for mental illness; however, insanity is a legal designation. NGRI acquittees are legally distinct from mentally ill offenders, and therefore follow a unique pathway within the criminal justice system.

The high prevalence of mental disorders within the general prison population suggests there will be mentally disordered persons in insane and non-insane offender pools.[12] Given that NGRI acquittees must meet the criteria for having a mental illness, one would expect all NGRI acquittees to be mentally ill. In a 1995 study, however, Cirincione and colleagues pooled data from eight different states treating persons adjudicated NGRI. Less than 60% of the NGRI acquittees (original sample of subjects submitting insanity pleas = 8,138) met the criteria for a major mental illness.

In terms of legal status, NGRI acquittees differ from offenders and non-offending mentally ill persons. They are acquitted for their crimes but then are referred to the state hospital system. The exact mechanism by which such a referral occurs differs from state to state. The disposition for each acquittee depends upon the local statute and the clinical status of the individual. In some cases, NGRI acquittees can be detained for durations far beyond the sentence they would have received had they been convicted for the original crime.[13] In other cases, they are assessed to be mentally healthy at sentencing and therefore released into the community with only outpatient treatment mandated.

Even though NGRI acquittees are a legally distinct group, health policy makers and clinicians often question whether they are a clinically unique group. In other words, should they receive services appropriate to mentally ill persons, other offenders, or do they demand services unique to their liminal position? The potential for post-discharge violence is necessarily at the center of any answer to this question. As stated in the introduction, administrators and clinicians carry the burden of providing services in the least restrictive setting possible while also protecting the community.[14]

Mental Illness and Violence
There is an enduring public perception that mentally ill persons are considerably more violent than non-mentally ill persons.[15] Selective and even distorted media reports and sensationalistic pop culture images have contributed to public stereotyping of the 'psycho killer.'[16] The degree to which mental illness is linked with violent behavior, however, is an empirical issue.

Some researchers have reported that mental disorder and violent behavior are related.[17] Others have found that controlling for demographic variables eliminates the observed link.[18] Still others suggest that mental disorder and violence are weakly associated;[19] and therefore, mental disorder is a relatively weak risk factor for violent behavior.[20]

Some researchers have focused less on broad mental disorders and more on specific symptoms (e.g. delusions that one is being followed, controlled or harmed) in order to obtain a more precise understanding of the link.[21] These preliminary studies have suggested that even isolated clinical variables are less effective than demographic variables (e.g. race, age, prior arrest history) in predicting future violence.[22] They suggest that an actuarial measure of demographic risk factors, coupled with clinical judgment and monitoring, is the best way to predict violent recidivism.[23]

Public Perception
Despite growing consensus within the research community concerning the modest association between the clinical variables studied and violence, the public continues to perceive a strong, causal relationship.[24] For many members of the public, to be mentally ill is to be a danger to society. This misperception seems to be particularly strong in relation to mentally ill criminal offenders.[25] The public seems to fear that mentally ill offenders will commit wanton acts of random violence at rates far beyond those of other offenders. Among offenders, NGRI acquittees typically evoke the strongest responses.[26] Perlin (1996) claims "that there [is] something about the insanity defense, and about the *persona* of the insanity defense pleader…that revolt[s] the general public; that the successful insanity pleader truly [is] one of the most 'despised' individuals in society."

Public perceptions do not merely influence the reception of NGRI acquittees within their communities. They also affect the legal and health policies that shape the delivery of services. One way to track this relationship is to identify whether cases receiving a great deal of publicity precipitate periods of widespread legislative reform. For example, the previously mentioned acquittal of John F. Hinkley Jr. resulted in legislative reforms in 65% of states.[27] There had been little substantive change in the empirical research, but legislators were influenced by the wide spread public outcry.

Researchers who have studied NGRI acquittees have challenged the following public perceptions: the insanity defense is commonly used and commonly successful;[28] insanity defendants tend to be wealthy persons benefiting from power and privilege;[29] and insanity defendants tend to serve short hospital terms and then return to the community rapidly.[30] These assumptions are now broadly accepted among researchers to be false. However, none of these perceptions is perhaps so damaging as the exaggerated link between NGRI acquittal and violent recidivism.[31] Given the intensity of individuals' fear and antipathy toward NGRI acquittees and the inordinate influence of public perception on policies within this realm (as demonstrated by the many legislative changes after the Hinkley acquittal), these misperceptions threaten to have dramatic impact. For example, since the Hinkley verdict, five states (MT, ID, UT, NV, and KS) have abolished the insanity defense.[32]

Veteran NGRI Acquittees
As the impact of the Iraq War endures, the need to study veterans grows in importance. A subset of NGRI acquittees have previously served in the military. When compared with non-veteran acquittees, veterans demonstrate disproportionate patterns of criminal activity and mental illness.[33] Varied and overlapping factors appear

to account for such behavioral and psychiatric disturbance. Most studies addressing violence and mental disorder among veterans have focused on the impact of Posttraumatic Stress Disorder.[34] PTSD has been associated with legal complications, interpersonal violence, psychological distress, unemployment, compromised physical health, and comorbid psychiatric disturbance.[35] However, PTSD is merely one constellation of symptoms among many that impact veterans uniquely. Anniversary reactions,[36] prior head injuries,[37] and poor reception upon returning from combat[38] have also been associated with more frequent and severe symptoms.

Veteran insanity defenses have commonly relied upon the assumption that PTSD and a specific subset of symptoms (e.g. anniversary reactions) profoundly impact the cognitive and volitional capacities of mentally disordered veterans.[39] The highly publicized 1982 case of the *People v. Wood* in Chicago, IL, typifies PTSD insanity defenses. Mr. Wood, a Vietnam veteran, was acquitted of shooting his factory foreman because the sounds within his workplace resembled combat noises and the aggressive behavior of his foreman triggered a combat-like response. Empirical attempts to link PTSD and criminal activity causally, however, have produced contradictory results, leaving veteran insanity defense claims shrouded in ambiguity.[40]

Few studies clarify the role of the insanity defense and the characteristics of persons adjudicated NGRI within the military. Lande (1990) argues that the dearth of data both causes and results from the military court system's imprecision in designating and disposing of insanity acquittees. More than a decade ago, he encouraged health services researchers to collect and analyze data that would allow policy shapers to make more informed decisions. Since then, numerous studies have highlighted the continuing confusion surrounding effective service delivery pathways for mentally ill veteran offenders. For example, Johnson and colleagues (1996) found that long-term intensive inpatient treatment, a common approach for treating chronic combat-related PTSD sufferers, may not only fail to ameliorate symptoms in a durable manner, but may result in worse long term clinical outcomes.

Lande (1990) argues that the most salient gap in the service delivery system designed to treat veteran NGRI acquittees concerns dispositional guidelines. After the acquittal, clinicians and administrators are forced to rely disproportionately on clinical judgment in designing effective interventions. The 1987 Uniform Code of Military Justice addresses insanity defenses but fails to clarify how acquittees should be treated and monitored after the trial. In a pilot study in 1991, Lande found that veterans appear both to use and succeed with the insanity defense at rates comparable to the general population. However, it is unclear whether veteran NGRI acquittees have unique clinical needs and particular vulnerabilities to recidivate once released into the community.

---

[1]Carroll, A., Lyall, M., & Forrester, A. (2004). Clinical hopes and public fears in forensic mental health. *Journal of Forensic Psychiatry and Psychology*, 15(3), 407-425.

[2]MacAuley, F. (1993). *Insanity, Psychiatry and Criminal Responsibility*. Dublin: Round Hall Press.

[3]Andoh, B. (1993). The M'Naghten rules—the story so far. *Medico-Legal Journal*, 61(1), 93-103.

[4]Matthews, S. (2004). Failed agency and the insanity defense. *International Journal of Law and Psychiatry*, 27(5), 413-424.

[5]Slobogin, C. (2003). The integrationist alternative to the insanity defense: Reflections on the exculpatory scope of mental illness in the wake of the Andrea Yates trial. *American Journal of Criminal Law*, 30(3), 315-341.

[6]American Law Institute. (1962). *Model penal code*. Proposed official draft. Philadelphia, §4.01.

[7]Matthews, S. (2004).

[8]Steadman, H. J., McGreevy, M. A., Morrissey, J. P., Callahan, L. A., Robbins, P. C., & Cirincione, C. (1993). *Before and after Hinckley: Evaluating insanity defense reform.* New York: Guilford.

[9]Callahan, L. A., Mayer, C., & Steadman, H. J. (1987). Post-Hinckley Insanity Defense Reforms in the United States, *Mental and Physical Disability Law Reporter, 11(1), 54-59.*

[10]Gutheil, T. G. (1999). A confusion of tongues: Competence, insanity, psychiatry, and the law. *Psychiatry Services*, 50(6), 767-773.

[11]Morse, S. J. (1999). Craziness and criminal responsibility. *Behavioral Sciences and the Law,* 17, 147-164.

[12]United States Department of Justice: Prison and jail inmates at midyear 2002. *Bureau of Justice Statistics*, NJC 198877, April 2003; Ditton P.M. (1999). Mental Health Treatment of Inmates and Probationers. Washington, DC, US Department of Justice; Teplin, L. A. (1990). The prevalence of severe mental disorder among male urban jail detainees: Comparison with the Epidemiologic Catchment Area program. *American Journal of Public Health*, 84, 290-293.

[13]Miller, R. D. (2002). Automatic commitment of insanity acquittees: Keeping up with the *Jones*? *Journal of Psychiatry and Law*, 30, 59-95.

[14]Bigelow, D. A., Bloom, J. D., Williams, M., & McFarland, B. H. (1999). An administrative model for close monitoring and managing high risk individuals. *Behavioral Sciences and the Law*, 17, 227-235.

[15]Arboleda-Florez, J. (1998). Mental illness and violence: An epidemiological appraisal of the evidence. *Canadian Journal of Psychiatry*, 43(10), 989-996; Phelan, L.C, & Link, B.G. (1998). The growing belief that people with mental illnesses are violent: The role of the dangerousness criterion for civil commitment.

Social Psychiatry and Psychiatric Epidemiology, 33(1), S7-S12; Monahan, J. (1992). Mental disorder and violent behavior: Perceptions and evidence. American Psychologist, 47, 511-521.

[16]Carroll, A., Lyall, M., & Forrester, A.; Lawrie, S. M. (1999). Stigmatization of psychiatric disorder. Psychiatric Bulletin, 23(3), 129-131; Mayer A., & Barry, D. D. (1992). Working with the media to destigmatize mental illness. Hospital and Community Psychiatry, 43, 77-78; Wahl. O. F. (1992). Mass media images of mental illness: A review of the literature. Journal of Community Psychology, 20, 343-352; National Mental Health Association (1983). Myths and realities: A report of the National Commission on the Insanity Defense. Arlington, VA: Author.

[17]Hodgins, S. & Mueller-Isberner, R. (2004). Preventing crime by people with schizophrenic disorders: The role of psychiatric services. British Journal of Psychiatry, 185, 245-250; Schanda, H., Knecht, G., Schreinzer, D., Stompe, Th., Ortwein-Swoboda, G., & Waldhoer, Th. (2004). Homicide and major mental disorders: A 25-year study. Acta Psychiatrica Scandinavica, 110, 98-107; Walsh, E., Buchanan, A., & Fahy, T. (2002). Violence and schizophrenia: Examining the evidence. British Journal of Psychiatry, 180, 490-495; Arseneault, L., Moffitt, T. E., Caspi, A., & Taylor, P. J. (2000). Mental disorders and violence in a total birth cohort: Results from the Dunedin study. Archives of General Psychiatry, 57, 979-986; Hodgins, S., Mednick, S. A., Brennan, P. A., Schulsinger, F., & Engberg, M. (1996). Mental disorder and crime: Evidence from a Danish birth cohort. Archives of General Psychiatry, 53(6), 489-496; Eronen, M., Hakola, P., & Tiihonen, J. (1996). Factors associated with homicide recidivism in a 13-year sample of homicide offenders in Finland, Psychiatric Services, 47, 403-406; Swanson, L.W. (1994). Mental disorder, substance abuse, and community violence: An epidemiological approach. In L. Monahan & H. Steadman (Eds.), Violence and mental disorder: Developments in risk assessment (pp. 101-136). Chicago: University of Chicago Press; Lindquist, P., & Allebeck, P. (1990). Schizophrenia and crime: A longitudinal follow-up of 644 schizophrenics in Stockholm. British Journal of Psychiatry, 157, 345-350. Schuerman, L. A., & Kobrin, S. (1984). Exposure of community mental health clients to the criminal justice system:

Client/criminal or patient/prisoner. In L.A. Teplin (Ed.), *Mental health and criminal justice* (pp. 87-118). Beverly Hills, CA: Sage; Sosowsky, L. (1980). Explaining the increased arrest rate among mental patients: A cautionary note. *American Journal of Psychiatry*, 137, 1602-1605; Swanson, J. W., Holzer, C. E., Ganju, V. K., & Jono, R. T. (1990). Violence and psychiatric disorder in the community: Evidence from the Epidemiologic Catchment Area surveys. *Hospital and Community Psychiatry*, 41, 761-770.

[18]Teplin, L. A., Abram, K. M., & McClelland, G. M. (1994). Does psychiatric disorder predict violent crime among released jail detainees? *American Psychologist*, 49(4), 335-342; Teplin, L. A. (1985). The criminality of the mentally ill: A dangerous misconception. *American Journal of Psychiatry*, 142, 593-599; Steadman, H. J., & Ribner, S. A. (1980). Changing perceptions of the mental health needs of inmates in local jail. *American Journal of Psychiatry*, 137, 1115-1116; Steadman, H. J., Cocozza, J. J., & Melick, M. E. (1978). Explaining the increased arrest rate among mental patients: The changing clientele of state hospitals. *American Journal of Psychiatry*, 135, 816-820.

[19]Monahan, J. (1993). Mental disorder and violence: Another look. In S. Hodgins (Ed.), *Mental disorder and crime* (pp.287-302). Newbury Park, CA: Sage.

[20]Teplin, L. A., Abram, K. M., & McClelland, G. M. (1994); Swanson, L.W. (1994); Link, B. G., Andrews, H., & Cullen, F. T. (1992). The violent and illegal behavior of mental patients reconsidered. *American Sociological Review*, 57, 275-292. Monahan, J. (1992). Mental disorder and violent behavior: Perceptions and evidence. *American Psychologist*, 47, 511-521. Swanson, J. W., Holzer, C. E., Ganju, V. K., & Jono, R. T. (1990).

[21]Appelbaum, P. S., Robbins, P. C., & Monahan, J. (2000). Violence and delusions: Data from the MacArthur Violence Risk Assessment Study. *American Journal of Psychiatry*, 157, 566-572; Rice, M. (1997). Violent offender research and implications for the criminal justice system. *American Psychologist*, 52(4), 414-423; Swanson, J. W., Borum, R., Swartz, M. S., Monahan, J. (1996). Psychotic symptoms and disorders and the risk of violent behavior in the community. *Criminal Behaviour and Mental Health,* 6(4), 309-329; Link, B., & Stueve, A. (1994). Psychotic symptoms and

the violent/illegal behavior of mental patients compared to community controls. In J. Monahan & H. Steadman (Eds.), *Violence and mental disorder: Developments in risk assessment* (pp.137-159). Chicago: University of Chicago Press.

[22]Phillips, H. K., Gray, N. S., MacCulloch, S. I., Taylor, J., Moore, S. C., Huckle, P., & MacCulloch, J. (2005). Risk assessment in offenders with mental disorders: Relative efficacy of personal demographic, criminal history, and clinical variables. Journal of Interpersonal Violence, 20(7), 833-847; Bonta, J., Hanson, K., & Law, M. (1998). The prediction of criminal and violent recidivism among mentally disordered offenders: A meta-analysis. *Psychological Bulletin.* 123(2), 123-142; Gendreau, P., Little, T., & Goggin, C. (1996). A meta-analysis of the predictors of adult offender recidivism: What works. *Criminology*, 34, 575-607; Andrews, D. A., & Bonta, J. (1994). *The psychology of criminal conduct.* Cincinnati, OH: Anderson Publishing Co.

[23]Haggard-Grann, U. & Gumpert, C. (2005). The violence relapse process – a qualitative analysis of high-risk situations and risk communication in mentally disordered offenders. *Psychology, Crime and Law*, 11(2), 199-222; Rice, M. (1997).

[24]Crisp, A., Gelder, M., Rix, S., & Meltzer, H. (2000). Stigmatisation of people with mental illnesses. *British Journal of Psychiatry*, 177, 4-7. Phelan, L.C, & Link, B.G. (1998). The growing belief that people with mental illnesses are violent: The role of the dangerousness criterion for civil commitment. *Social Psychiatry and Psychiatric Epidemiology*, 33(1), S7-S12.

[25]Morrall, P. (2000). *Madness and Murder.* London: Whurr. Shah, S. (1990). The mentally disordered offenders: Some issues of policy and planning. In E.H. Cox-Feith, & B.N.W. de Smit (Eds.), *Innovations in mental health legislation and government policy: A European perspective.* The Hague: The Netherlands Ministry of Justice. Steadman, H., & Cocozza, J. (1978). Selective reporting and the public's misconceptions of the criminally insane. *Public Opinion Quarterly*, 41, 523-533.

[26]Hans, V. P., & Slater, D. (1983). John Hinckley, Jr. and the insanity defense: The public's verdict. *Public Opinion Quarterly*, 47(2), 202-212.

[27]Steadman, H. J., McGreevy, M. A., Morrissey, J. P., Callahan, L. A., Robbins, P. C., & Cirincione, C. (1993). Hans, V. P., & Slater, D. (1983).

[28]Blau, G. L. & Pasewark, R. A. (1994). Satutory changes and the insanity defense: Seeking the perfect insane person. *Law and Psychology Review*, 18, 69. Pasewark, R. A., Seidenzahl, D., & Pantle, M. (1981). Opinions concerning criminality among mental patients. *Journal of Community Psychology*, 9(4), 367-370.

[29]Linhorst, D. M., Hunsucker, L., & Parker, L. D. (1998). An examination of gender and racial differences among Missouri insanity acquittees. *Journal of the American Academy of Psychiatry and the Law*, 26(3), 411-424; Seig, A., Ball, E., & Menninger, L. A. (1995). A comparison of female versus male insanity aquittees in Colorado. *Bulletin of the American Academy of Psychiatry and the Law*, 23(4), 523-532; Zonana, H. V., Wells, J. A., Getz, M. A., & Buchanan, J. A. (1990). The NGRI registry: Initial analyses of data collected on Connecticut insanity acquittees: I. *Bulletin of the American Academy of Psychiatry and the Law*, 18(2), 115-128; Bogenberger, R. P., Pasewark, R. A., Gudeman, H., & Beiber, S. L. (1987). Follow-up of insanity acquittees in Hawaii. *International Journal of Law and Psychiatry*, 10, 283-295. Boehnert, C. E. (1985). Psychological and demographic factors associated with individuals using the insanity defense. *Journal of Psychiatry and Law*, 13(1-2), 9-31; Steadman, H. J. (1980). Insanity acquittals in New York State, 1965-1978. *American Journal of Psychiatry*, 137(3), 321-326; Pasewark, R. A., Pantle M. L., & Steadman, H. J. (1979). The insanity plea in New York State, 1965-1976. *New York State Bar Journal*, 186-225.

[30]Miller, R. D. (2002); Arboleda-Florez, J., Holley, H., & Crisanti, A. (1998). Mental illness and violence. *International Medical Journal*, 5(1), 3-8. Pasewark, R. A. (1986). A review of research on the insanity defense. *Annals of the American Academy of Psychiatry and the Social Sciences*, 484, 100-115. Steadman, H. J. (1985). Empirical research on the insanity defense. *Annals of the American Academy of Psychiatry and the Social Sciences*, 477, 58-71.

[31]Perlin, M. (1996). Myths, realities, and the political world: The anthropology of insanity defense attitudes. *Bulletin of the American Academy of Psychiatric Law*, 24(1), 5-26.

[32]Borum, R., & Fulero, S. M. (1999). Empirical research on the insanity defense and attempted reforms: Evidence toward informed policy. *Law and Human Behavior*, 23(1), 1999.

[33]Higgins, S. A. (1991). Post-traumatic stress disorder and its role in the defense of Vietnam veterans. *Law and Psychology Review*, 15, 259-276.

[34]Zatzick, D. F., Maramar, C. R., Weiss, D. S., Browner, W. S., Metzler, T. J., Golding, J. M., et al.(1997). Posttraumatic Stress Disorder and functioning and quality of life outcomes in a nationally representative sample of male Vietnam veterans. *American Journal of Psychiatry*, 154(12), 1690-1695.

[35]Fontana, A., Schwartz, L. S., & Rosenheck, R. (1997). Posttraumatic Stress Disorder among female Vietnam veterans: A causal model of etiology. *American Journal of Public Health*, 87(2), 169-175; Zatzick, D. F., Maramar, C. R., Weiss, D. S., Browner, W. S., Metzler, T. J., Golding, J. M., et al.(1997); Kulka R. A., Schlenger W. E., Fairbank J.A., Hough R.L., Jordan B. K., Marmar C. R., Weiss D.S. (1990). *Trauma and the Vietnam war generation: Report of findings from the national Vietnam veterans readjustment study*. New York: Brunner/Mazel; Friedman, M.J., & Schnurr, P.P. (1995). The relationship between trauma, post-traumatic stress disorder, and physical health. In M. J. Friedman, D. S. Charney, & A. Y. Deutch (Eds.), *Neurobiological and clinical consequences of stress: From normal adaption to PTSD (pp. 507-524)*. Philadelphia: Lippincott-Raven.

[36]Morgan, C. A., Hill, S., Fox, P., Kingham, P., & Southwick, M. (1999). Anniversary reactions in gulf war veterans: A follow-up inquiry 6 years after the war. *American Journal of Psychiatry*, 156, 1075-1079.

[37]Grafman, J., Schwab, K., Warden, D., Pridgen, A., Brown, H. R., & Salazar, A. M. (1996). Frontal lobe injuries, violence, and aggression: A report of the Vietnam Head Injury Study. *Neurology*, 46, 1231-1738.

[38]Pilisuk, M. (1975). The legacy of the Vietnam veteran. *Journal of Social Issues*, 31(4), 3-12.

[39]Higgins, S. A. (1991).

[40]Slovenko, R. (2004). The watering down of PTSD in criminal law. Journal of Psychiatry and Law, 32, 411-438. Sparr, L. F., & Atkinson, R. M. (1986). Posttraumatic stress disorder as an insanity defense: Medicolegal quicksand. *American Journal of Psychiatry*, 143(5), 608-613. Packer, I. K. (1983). Post-traumatic stress disorder and the insanity defense: A critical analysis. *Journal of Psychiatry and Law*, 11(2), 125-136.

CHAPTER 2

NGRI Research Programs

Studies of NGRI Criminal Recidivism
How many NGRI acquittees released into the community
will commit crimes and how can we distinguish the
recidivates from the others? For the last fifty years,
researchers have been trying to answer these questions
using empirical methods. The first empirical study of
criminal recidivism among a pure sample of NGRI
acquittees was conducted in 1966 by Morrow and Peterson.
Since then, a more sophisticated understanding of
recidivism patterns has been built upon a relatively
disjointed foundation. Though the studies that make up this
foundation have often been methodologically sound, they
have been limited by inconsistencies across projects. For
example, the following trends have impeded the integration
of results: the dependent variable (rates of criminal
recidivism) has been operationalized variably; the criteria
used to identify subjects depend upon the presiding
regional insanity rules and therefore differ from state to
state; furthermore, researchers have calculated recidivism
rates using vastly differing follow up periods. Each of
these issues limits one's ability to integrate results across
studies and therefore make broader statements about the
balance between personal freedom and community safety.

In an attempt to integrate the present literature, I have
summarized the results of twenty studies that met the
criteria for this review (see Table 1). I chose studies that

isolated NGRI acquittees from other potential subjects and clearly defined the ways in which the dependent variable was operationalized. The majority of these studies have been described in other reviews;[41] however, these reviews have either included studies that violated the criteria for the present review or compared studies without identifying pertinent confounding variables (e.g. variable definitions of insanity from state to state).

Numerous studies that were excluded from the present review are commonly cited in the literature.[42] One group of studies was eliminated because of overly broad sampling that either included mentally ill offenders,[43] persons deemed incompetent to stand trial,[44] or vague categories of subjects such as "offender patients."[45] These populations may differ in important ways from pure samples of NGRI acquittees. For example, mentally ill offenders differ from NGRI acquittees in that they have been exposed to the criminal subculture in jails and prisons and have not necessarily received clinical treatment.[46]

The second group of studies did not specify clear methods for operationalizing the dependent variable. For example, Yesavage and colleagues (1986) measured criminal recidivism by assessing re-admittance into the hospital facility that treats persons found not criminally responsible in France. It is unclear how persons, who committed post-discharge crimes and were convicted, were measured. It is also unclear whether persons who were re-admitted for non-criminal behavior (e.g. decompensation) were distinguished from those persons who actually recidivated. Therefore, without a more precise description of the ways in which patients move through the mental health and criminal justice systems, the measure of the dependent variable is unclear.

Table 1: Studies in NGRI criminal recidivism

Study	Site	N	Follow-Up	Re-Arrests	Re-Arrests for Violence	Correlates
Morrow et al., 1966	MO	35	< 6 yrs	13/35 Convictions 37.1%	2/35 Convictions 5.7%	Prior convictions
Pasewark et al., 1979	NY	107	< 11.2 yrs	21/107 19.6%	NA	Prior arrest, male
Pantle et al., 1980	NY	37	5.5 – 11.5 yrs	9/37 24.3%	NA	Male
Pasewark et al., 1982	NY	33	3 – 6 yrs	5/33 15.2%	NA	Prior arrest, male
Pasewark et al., 1982	NY	148	5 – 10 yrs	Released: 38/133 28.5% AWOL: 3/15 20.0%	NA	Male

Table Continues

Table 1: Studies in NGRI criminal recidivism -- Continued

Study	Site	N	Follow-Up	Re-Arrests		Re-Arrests for Violence	Correlates
Rogers et al., 1982	OR	165	< 3 yrs	17/165	10.3%	8/165 4.8%	NA
Rogers et al., 1984	OR	295	1.2–5.1 yrs	39/295	13.2%	15/295 5.1%	NA
Spodak et al., 1984	MD	86	5–15 yrs (μ=9.5)	48/86	55.8%	12/86 14.0%	No hospitalization
Cavanaugh et al., 1985	IL	44	1–2 yrs	2/44	4.5%	0/44 0.0%	NA
Bloom et al., 1986	OR	123	< 3 yrs	CR: 31/123 Contacts Post: 53/123 Contacts	25.2% 43.0%	NA	Discharge from conditional release, prior arrest, younger
Bloom et al, 1986	OR	67	2 yrs	11/67	16.4%	NA	NA
Bogenberger et al., 1987	HI	107	8–14.5 yrs	72/107	67.3%	NA	Hospitalization

Table Continues

Table 1: Studies in NGRI criminal recidivism -- Continued

Study	Site	N	Follow-Up	Re-Arrests		Re-Arrests for Violence	Correlates
Beiber et al., 1988	NY	132	5–10 yrs	38/132 28.9%		NA	Prior arrest, psychotic d.o. index crime homicide
Lamb et al., 1988	CA	79	3.8 yrs	25/79 31.6%		18/79 22.8%	Revocation of outpatient treatment, poor supervision
Silver et al., 1989	MD	127	7–17 yrs (μ=10)	2 yr: 43 /127 5 yr: 69/127 17 yr: 83/127	33.8% 54.3% 65.8%	NA	NA
Nicholson et al, 1991	OK	30	2.75 yrs	All: 10/30 AWOL: 4/5 Treated: 3/16 Untreated: 3/9	33.3% 80.0% 18.8% 33.3%	NA	Untreated (released at initial review) or AWOL
McGreevy et al., 1991	NY	331	3.8 yrs	75/331 22.7%		NA	NA

Table Continues

Table 1: Studies in NGRI criminal recidivism -- Continued

Study	Site	N	Follow-Up	Re-Arrests	Re-Arrests for Violence	Correlates
Rice et al., 1991	CAN	253	μ=78.2	103/253 40.7%	49/244 20.1%	Less recidivistic than matched offenders
Stafford et al., 1997	OH	38	NA	5/38 13.2%	NA	NA
Luettgen et al., 1998	CAN	74	6.7 yrs	8/74 Convictions 10.8%	2/74 Convictions 2.7%	Male, younger, prior convictions, schizophrenia substance abuse
Kravitz et al., 1999	IL	43	4.9 – 18.4 yrs	8/43 18.6%	5/43 11.6%	Poor social adjustment, living situation, or outcome of most recent clinical episode

The study of NGRI criminal recidivism has often occurred in the context of research programs. These programs have ranged from groups of colleagues at separate institutions working collaboratively (e.g. Steadman, Pasewark, and Pantle in New York) to staffs of researchers who are more closely embedded in the systems they are studying (e.g. Bloom, Rogers, Manson and Williams at Oregon Health Sciences University who are affiliated with Oregon's Psychiatric Security Review Board). By approaching these research programs as loosely and not so loosely defined units, one can more easily monitor the influence of potentially confounding variables (e.g. regional differences in insanity statutes). I therefore will use the published papers about New York State as a case study to demonstrate the progression of one loosely organized program of research. All twenty NGRI studies in the present review are summarized in Appendix A and even more succinctly depicted in Table 1.

New York State

A series of studies of NGRI criminal recidivism have been conducted in New York State at significant moments in the development of a comprehensive service delivery system. In order to understand the relevance of these studies, it is important to highlight two legislative changes that significantly affected the NGRI service pathways. In 1971, the criminal procedures surrounding the insanity defense were changed in New York thereby shifting responsibility from the mental health facility operated by the Department of Correctional Services to civil mental hospitals.[47] The change in criminal procedures altered the entity responsible for assessing and treating defendants upon acquittal.

In 1980, a second piece of legislation altered a later stage in the treatment pathways. New York State's Insanity Defense Reform Act outlined the procedures by which NGRI acquittees were to be conditionally released into the community.[48] The process for obtaining a release is ten-tiered and proceeds in chronological order as follows: "The treating clinician recommends conditional release, which is followed by reviews by the treatment team, the hospital forensic committee, the hospital clinical director, the hospital executive director, the state forensic committee, a forensic specialist in the Office of Mental Health, a psychiatrist, the district attorney, and finally the judge."[49] Though the process is arduous, it provides clinicians and administrators with additional service pathways. Instead of either holding acquittees in the hospital or releasing them into the community without any treatment mandates, mental health professionals can release acquittees into a community based treatment setting that includes frequent monitoring, treatment, and efficient revocation procedures. A variety of outpatient treatments, structured living assignments, and psychotropic medications can be mandated as part of the conditional release.

These legislative reforms altered the treatment pathways along which NGRI acquittees move and thereby distinguished three groups of acquittees (see Table 2). Subjects followed from 1965 to 1971 were channeled through the correctional hospital system and could only be unconditionally released into the community (Group1). Subjects followed from 1971 to 1980 were channeled through the civil psychiatric hospital system and could only be unconditionally released into the community (Group 2). Finally, subjects followed after 1980 were channeled through the civil psychiatric hospital system and released into the community through conditional release programs (Group 3). Pasewark and colleagues (1979) conducted the first pure NGRI recidivism study in New York State. They followed 107 NGRI acquittees for up to 11.2 years spanning the years before and after the shift from correctional to civil hospitals (Groups 1 and 2). They found that 21 of the 107 acquittees (19.6%) were re-arrested. In fact, many of the recidivates were re-arrested multiple times (3.2 arrests per person on average), and 25% of the crimes were violent. Given the lengthy follow up period, the re-arrest rates were considered relatively low. However, the high proportion of violent crimes was discouraging.

Table 2: Pathway characteristics of New York State NGRI system

Group	Time Period	Hospital System	Release Type
1	1965 – 1971	Correctional	Unconditional
2	1971 – 1980	Civil	Unconditional
3	1980 and beyond	Civil	Conditional

Pantle and colleagues (1980) later conducted a study focusing exclusively on acquittees who were channeled through the correctional hospital system before the 1971 legislative changes (Group 1). They used a follow up period ranging from 5.5 to 11.5 years. Nine (24.3%) of the NGRI acquittees were arrested. Less than 14% of the charges were for violent crimes. Therefore, a sample of acquittees from Groups 1 and 2 combined had a comparable re-arrest rate to a sample of acquittees solely from Group 1. The combined group committed a higher proportion of violent crimes however. Recognizing the limitations of extrapolating from studies that may have significant methodological differences (e.g. variable follow up periods), it appears that hospitalization within the correctional hospital facilities as opposed to the civil hospital system may lead to less violent post-discharge recidivism. Such a conclusion demands further study however.

The Pantle study not only focused on the acquittees funneled through the correctional hospital system (Group 1), but also compared these NGRI acquittees with a matched group of convicted felons. The NGRI acquittees and felons had comparable arrest rates; however, the felons were more commonly arrested for crimes against persons. Therefore, though the acquittees were comparably recidivistic, they were less violent in their re-offending.

Pasewark and colleagues (1982) filled in the gap left open by the Pantle study. They focused exclusively on the acquittees who were tracked through the civil hospital system before the time of conditional release (Group 2). They matched 33 NGRI acquittees with convicted felons and followed them for 3 to 6 years post-discharge. They found that 5 of the 33 NGRI acquittees (15.2%) were re-arrested. Once again, no significant differences between the convicted felons and the NGRI acquittees were found. It is difficult to compare the rates of recidivism found in this study with the two prior studies because of significant differences in follow up periods.

Pasewark and colleagues (1982) published an additional study of Group 2 acquittees in New York State using a larger sample and longer follow-up period. These changes in scope would be sufficient justification for conducting another study; however, they also performed an intra-group comparison. For 5 to 10 years, they followed 133 NGRI acquittees released into the community through formal pathways and 15 NGRI acquittees who escaped from the hospital. Thirty-eight of the 133 released acquittees (28.5%) and 3 of the 15 escaped acquittees (20.0%) were re-arrested. These results were considered discouraging given that patients who escaped, and therefore were largely untreated, appeared to be less recidivistic than offenders who moved through the normal treatment and release pathways. Since the reasons for this unexpected finding were not addressed empirically, one is left to offer hypotheses. The most discouraging and seemingly improbable interpretation is that the escaped acquittees were less recidivistic simply because they spent less time in the hospital system. It is more probable that either the escaped acquittees experienced additional pressure not to recidivate because of their need to avoid the authorities or that more of the escaped acquittees fled New York State and therefore their criminal activity went undetected.

McGreevy and colleagues (1991) studied the Group 3 acquittees who had been tracked through the conditional release programs. They followed 331 NGRI acquittees for an average of 3.8 years. The conditional release mandates included a combination of outpatient therapy, specialized housing and psychotropic medications. Seventy-five acquittees (22.7%) were arrested during the follow up period. The vast majority of arrests were for minor infractions (92% D felonies or less); however, no data concerning the proportion of individuals committing violent crimes were offered. Once again, it is difficult to compare arrest rates across studies because of the probability of confounding variables (e.g. offenders in general in the 1980s may have tended to be more recidivistic than in the 1970s). Assuming the results are reliable, the conditional release program did not appear to be successful in reducing the overall re-arrest rate though it may have reduced the proportion of violent re-offending.

Lastly, Beiber and colleagues (1988) conducted additional analyses on a sample of 133 acquittees used in an earlier study.[50] Using stepwise discriminant procedures, they calculated structure coefficients for numerous variables identified as predictors of recidivism in the literature. The most robust predictors were the following factors: number of prior arrests (0.68), severity of those arrests (0.61), and either a psychotic diagnosis (0.58) or an index offense of homicide (0.51). In two prior studies,[51] prior arrests were associated with increased likelihood of criminal recidivism. The only correlate to appear in the New York literature even more commonly was male gender.[52] Therefore, males with criminal histories appear to be the most vulnerable acquittees to recidivate. In terms of actually predicting who would be re-arrested, Beiber and colleagues were more successful in predicting non-recidivism (86.2% correct predictions) than recidivism (52.6% correct predictions).

Broader Results
The results from the New York studies are part of a more expansive literature. Both Appendix A and Table 1 outline the results of each of the twenty studies included in the present review. The following results are particularly noteworthy.

Rates of Recidivism. There was a great deal of variability among the rates of recidivism calculated in the twenty studies (see Table 3). In the majority of studies, between

15 to 40% of subjects recidivated. However, there were many examples of recidivism rates outside of this range. In Hawaii, Bogenberger and colleagues found that nearly 68% of the 107 acquittees they followed recidivated. At the lower limit, Cavanaugh and colleagues found that less than 5% of their 44 subjects in Illinois recidivated. Are these results the product of differences in the sample populations, service delivery systems, or methods? Numerous factors, such as the length of the follow up period, criteria used in the state insanity statutes, or measures of criminal recidivism, varied between studies. For example, Bogenberger and colleagues used nearly a 15 year follow up period whereas Cavanaugh and colleagues followed their subjects between 1 and 2 years. Varying follow up periods undoubtedly influenced the results.[53] However, this factor does not explain the entirety of the variation.

Table 3: Range of NGRI criminal recidivism rates

Variable	Range	Study	Result
Re-arrest	Maximum	Bogenberger et al., 1987	67.3%
Re-arrest	Maximum	Silver et al., 1989	65.8%
Re-arrest	Minimum	Cavanaugh et al., 1985	4.5%
Re-arrest	Minimum	Rogers et al., 1982	10.3%
Violent Re-arrest	Maximum	Lamb et al., 1988	22.8%
Violent Re-arrest	Minimum	Cavanaugh et al., 1985	0.0%

As one would expect, the rates of violent recidivism were considerably lower than the overall recidivism rates. The upper limit of the range was obtained by Lamb and colleagues in California. They found that more than 22%

of their 79 subjects were re-arrested for violent crimes during the 3.8 year follow up period. The lower limit was again defined by Cavanaugh and colleagues in Illinois. They followed 44 subjects for 1 to 2 years and found that none of them had committed violent offenses.

Table 4: Correlates of criminal recidivism

Correlates of Recidivism	Studies
Prior Criminal History	Morrow, 1966; Pasewark, 1979; Pasewark, 1982; Bloom, 1986; Beiber, 1988; Luettgen, 1998
Male	Pasewark, 1979; Pasewark, 1980; Pasewark, 1982; Luettgen, 1998
Younger	Bloom, 1986; Luettgen, 1998
Psychotic Disorder	Beiber, 1988; Luettgen, 1998
Comorbid Substance Abuse	Luettgen, 1998
Poor Social Adjustment	Kravitz, 1999
Poor Living Arrangement	Kravitz, 1999
Poor Outcome of Most Recent Clinical Episode	Kravitz, 1999

Correlates of Recidivism. One of the primary functions of these studies is to identify factors associated with recidivism that could serve as predictors.   As was mentioned in the New York case study, prior criminal history was the most robust predictor of recidivism.   This result was replicated in Missouri, Oregon, and Canada.[54] Though the New York studies identified a strong association between male gender and a tendency to recidivate, this result was only replicated in the Canadian study.[55] Younger age,[56] psychotic disorder,[57] comorbid substance abuse,[58] poor social adjustment, poor living situation, and poor outcome of most recent clinical episode were also associated with recidivism in at least one study.[59] However, the only predictor that was replicated in at least three research programs was criminal history.

Table 5: Comparisons of criminal recidivism rates between NGRI acquittees and other groups

Study	Comparison Group	Result
Luettgen	General population	Comparable re-arrest
Morrow	Prison population	Comparable re-arrest
Nicholson	Treated/Released/AWOL	AWOL > Release > Treated
Pantle	Convicted felons	Comparable re-arrest, Felons more violent
Pasewark, 1982	Convicted felons	Comparable re-arrest
Rice	Matched offenders	NGRIS less recidivistic
Silver	Prison parolees	Comparable re-arrest
Silver	Mentally ill parolees	NGRIs less recidivistic

Comparisons Between Groups. The first stage in studying NGRI release patterns is understanding the extent of the recidivism. Once basic rates have been calculated, one can begin to compare rates between groups in order to determine relative levels of risk. By obtaining such information, treatment pathways can be tailored to differing propensities. For example, if mentally ill offenders are consistently more recidivistic than NGRI acquittees, these offenders can immediately be referred to a service delivery pathway with more restrictions and more frequent monitoring.

NGRI acquittees were most commonly compared with the following prison samples: convicted felons,[60] prison parolees,[61] mentally ill offenders[62] and random samples of prisoners.[63] Each of these studies demonstrated that NGRI acquittees had recidivism rates statistically comparable to each of these groups with the following exceptions. Silver and colleagues found that the mentally ill offenders were more recidivistic than the NGRI group. Furthermore, though Pantle and colleagues found that the convicted felons and NGRI acquittees had comparable recidivism rates, they found that the felons were more violent.

Sources of Variation
As is demonstrated in Table 3, the rates of recidivism obtained in the studies vary considerably. This variability is most likely due to some combination of real differences between populations and methodological differences between studies. In an attempt to understand better the combination of factors involved, numerous researchers have reviewed clinical and demographic factors that could possibly be associated with recidivism.[64] Within this section, I will briefly summarize the findings from previous

reviews, identify the range of characteristics within the present review (see Table 6), and highlight those factors that have been linked with criminal recidivism.

Table 6: Range of demographic characteristics of NGRI acquittees

Variable	Minimum	Maximum
Age	30 years old (Bloom et al., 1986)	36 years old (Pasewark et al., 1979)
Criminal History	42% previously arrested (Beiber et al., 1988)	100% previously arrested Bogenberger et al., 1987
Diagnosis	46% psychotic disorder (Cavanaugh & Wasyliw, 1985)	90% psychotic disorder (Lamb et al., 1988)
Education	median grade = 9th (Morrow & Peterson, 1966)	median grade = 13th (Kravitz et al., 1999)
Employment History	14% employed (Nicholson et al., 1991)	88% employed (Kravitz et al., 1999)
Gender	64% male (Cavanaugh & Wasyliw, 1985)	100% male (Silver et al., 1989)
Hospitalization History	22% previously hosp. (Bogenberger et al., 1987)	95% previously hosp. (Nicholson et al., 1991)
Marital Status	8% married (Bloom & Williams, 1994)	57% married (Cavanaugh & Wasyliw, 1985)
Race/Ethnicity	17% Caucasian (Cavanaugh & Wasyliw, 1985)	87% Caucasian (Bloom & Williams, 1994)

Gender

As of 1998, 90% of the jail population in the United States was male.[65] Similar to the larger offending population, the majority of NGRI acquittees are male.[66] In most studies of NGRI characteristics, the ratio of males to females is approximately 10:1.[67] The recidivism studies in the present review vary considerably in the distribution of males and females. The proportion of males in the samples varied from 100%[68] to 64%.[69]

In a comparison of male and female NGRI acquittees, Seig and colleagues (1995) demonstrated that female acquittees tended to be older, have less violent criminal histories, and shorter lengths of detention despite usually having committed more serious index offenses. Previous reviews of the literature on violence in psychiatric populations have demonstrated that males are consistently more likely to be violent.[70] In five studies included in the present review, the authors suggest that males are more likely to be re-arrested than females.[71] Each of these results suggests that differences in the gender distribution among samples may lead to substantive differences in studies of correlates. However, the small samples of females limits the external validity of such claims. Furthermore, four out of the five studies that found a correlation between gender and recidivism were conducted within New York State. Therefore, not only the distribution but the impact of gender on the results may vary according to region.

Age

The mean age of NGRI acquittee samples is consistently in the 30s. In the present studies, the mean age varied from 30 years old[72] to 36 years old.[73] It is unclear whether persons in their thirties are more likely to be successful in using the insanity defense or more likely to both be insane and commit a crime.[74] Luettgen and colleagues (1998) found that persons who were at least 3.9 years younger than the sample mean (34.1 years old) were more likely to be re-convicted. This finding is consistent with reviews of the literature on violence in psychiatric populations.[75]

Race/Ethnicity

Whereas the general prison population is disproportionately African-American relative to the population at large, the NGRI acquittee population tends to include more whites.[76] In studies directly comparing NGRI samples with general prison populations, the NGRI samples consistently demonstrate higher proportions of whites. For example, in a Connecticut study, 80% of the NGRI sample was white compared to 55% of the incarcerated group.[77] There seem to be no consistent racial differences in the success rates of insanity defendants therefore the source of this variation is unknown.[78] Within the recidivism studies included in the present review, the proportion of whites in the sample varied from 17%[79] to 66%.[80] The Hawaiian sample[81] had the most racial variation thereby reflecting the racial diversity within the broader Hawaiian population. No link between racial/ethnicity and recidivism was found.

Marital Status

The proportion of married acquittees varied from 14%[82] to 57%[83] within the studies in this review. Though past reviews of the clinical and demographic characteristic of insanity defendants have demonstrated that NGRI acquittees tend to be unmarried,[84] marital status has not been associated with criminal recidivism.

Education

Similar to most populations of offenders, NGRI acquittees typically have had limited educational backgrounds. When compared with samples of incarcerated persons, they typically have higher mean years in school; however, they still tend to have less schooling than the general population.[85] For example, in a comparison of NGRI acquittees and a random sample of incarcerated persons, the NGRI acquittees averaged 11 years schooling compared to the incarcerated samples' 9 years schooling.[86] Contrary to public perceptions, most studies suggest that the majority of insanity defendants have not completed high school. Within the present review, the median grade completed ranged from 9[th][87] to one year of college.[88] No researchers identified educational status as a factor that could be correlated with criminal recidivism however.

Employment Status

Insanity acquittees tend to have sporadic work histories.[89] Within the recidivism studies, the proportion of acquittees employed at the time of the index crime varied from 14%[90] to 88%.[91] Employment history was not correlated with criminal recidivism in any studies.

Criminal History

The range of acquittees previously arrested ranged from 42%[92] to 100%.[93] The range for persons who previously were arrested for violent offenses was even broader. Pasewark and colleagues (1982) found that 13% of acquittees had previously been arrested for violent crimes whereas Lamb and colleagues found that a much larger proportion had violent criminal histories (84%).

A variety of studies have demonstrated relationships between criminal history and post-release arrest.[94] In past reviews of violence assessments among psychiatric patients, violent criminal histories have repeatedly been linked with future acts of violence.[95] In fact, this factor appears to be the most reliable correlate of criminal recidivism. Within the twenty studies included in the review, the following results were obtained:

- Morrow and colleagues (1966) found that acquittees who had been convicted either of multiple "economic offenses" (including index and prior charges) or any felony offense were more likely to be convicted again.

- In two studies, Pasewark and colleagues (1979; 1982) found that acquittees who had been arrested prior to the index charge were more likely to be arrested post-release.

- Beiber and colleagues (1988) replicated Pasewark's results and additionally found that acquittees whose index crime was murder were more likely to be arrested after being released into the community.

- Luettgen and colleagues (1998) found that acquittees who had been convicted of any crime prior to their index offense were more likely to be convicted post-release.

These results would be particularly noteworthy if NGRI acquittees tended to have more violent criminal histories than other groups. The following two studies suggest that such a trend occurs:

- Randolph and Pasewark (1984) compared the arrest histories for NGRI acquittees with the general population in Wyoming. They found that arrests for the following violent offenses were over-represented in the NGRI group: homicide (16.2% v. 3%); rape (5.9% v. 0.4%); other sex crimes (4.4% v. 0.8%); and robbery (2.9% v. 0.4%).

- Phillips and Pasewark (1980) suggest that NGRI acquittees have more serious offense histories even when compared with a random sample of incarcerated persons.

Diagnosis
NGRI acquittees tend to be diagnosed with psychotic disorders.[96] For example, in a broad review of 758 acquittees, Bloom and Williams (1994) found that approximately 60% of the sample was diagnosed with some type of psychotic disorder. Similar results have been obtained in numerous other studies.[97] However, these diagnoses are often accompanied by secondary personality and substance use disorders.[98]

As demonstrated with numerous other factors, there was a wide range of diagnoses present in the recidivism studies. The proportion of acquittees diagnosed with psychotic disorders varied from 46%[99] to 90%.[100] Smaller ranges were present for mood, personality, and substance use disorders. Though research concerning the relationship between diagnosis and violence has suggested that psychotic disorders, substance use disorders, and violence are linked,[101] no diagnostic factors were linked with criminal recidivism in the present review.

Hospitalization History
The rates of previous hospitalization varied considerably among studies. In Hawaii, Bogenberger and colleagues (1987) found that 22% of the acquittees had been previously hospitalized. However, Nicholson and colleagues (1991) found that more than 95% of acquittees were hospitalized prior to being acquitted. Hospitalization prior to the index offense was not linked with criminal recidivism in any of the studies. However, hospitalization as part of the treatment plan after-acquittal was linked to recidivism in two studies. Bogenberger's study suggested that those persons who were hospitalized before being released into the community were more likely to be re-arrested. Contradicting these results, Spodak and colleagues (1984) found that acquittees who were released into the community immediately after acquittal, rather than being hospitalized for a period of time, were more likely to be re-arrested. Given these competing claims, it is difficult to make any firm conclusions. Furthermore, the mean length of post-acquittal hospitalization varied considerably between studies. The acquittees in Kravitz and colleagues' study stayed on average only 68 days whereas the

acquittees in Morrow's study stayed on average 960 days. It seems likely that this variance is largely due to the shift toward outpatient treatment in the broader health care industry.

Methodological Issues
Construct Validity
Insanity is a legal term. Though lay persons and professionals often consider it a psychiatric label, it lacks clarity and precision within the realm of mental health categorization.[102] An insane person meets specific criteria defined by the state insanity statute. Therefore, even though these criteria resemble diagnostic criteria used by mental health professionals, the clinical implications of such a designation are vague.

When examining insanity acquittees, what construct is being studied? Contrary to public opinion, it is not a psychological but rather a legal construct.[103] Even within the legal community, insanity means different things in different states. Since the federal government passed the Insanity Defense Reform Act in 1984, the criteria have become more standardized; however, there is still considerable variation. Therefore, to study an NGRI acquittee in one state may not be the same as studying one in another state, thereby challenging the construct validity of such research.

If insanity is not a psychiatric construct, what is the significance of insanity for the mental health system? Mental health professionals participate and even occupy a central role in insanity proceedings. Although the judge or jury ultimately adjudicates the case, their judgments rarely contradict the results from mental health assessments.[104] Furthermore, it is illegal to detain an acquittee for punitive reasons after acquittal (Foucha v. Louisiana, 504 U.S. 71 (1992)). Therefore, the locus of responsibility often shifts from the criminal justice to the mental health system once the case has been adjudicated.

There is research that demonstrates that the transferring of responsibility between the systems may not be happening as efficiently as it should. For example, index offense severity has been associated with length of detention in many studies.[105] It is possible that more severe index offenses are associated with more severe mental illness and therefore should be correlated with longer periods of detention, or more severe index offenses are associated with a greater need to protect the public and increasing estimates of dangerousness. However, these results also raise the possibility that punitive models of containment are being employed despite their potential violation of individuals' rights.

Once persons are acquitted NGRI, they can be hospitalized or placed on conditional release if they are dangerously mentally ill. This protective measure is consistent with the dangerousness to others and dangerousness to self criteria that commonly influences hospital admissions. These interventions also may be deemed clinically appropriate in certain cases. However, the assessment should ultimately be conducted by mental health professionals in such instances.[106] At the heart of these assessments is the attempt to translate insanity into clinically meaningful criteria and diagnoses. Until such a translation occurs, it is difficult to assess the validity of the insanity construct for mental health professionals.

External Validity
Small Sample Sizes and Low Base Rates. The majority of NGRI recidivism studies in the present review used less than 90 subjects. If one estimates that 20% of a 90 person sample would be re-arrested in a three year period, the recidivistic group would consist of 18 persons. One has insufficient power to conduct complicated analyses with such a sample. Rather, one must make simple comparisons that do not account for the multiplicity of factors potentially influencing the dependent variable. Given the complex position that NGRI acquittees hold at the boundaries of the criminal justice and mental health systems, simplified analyses will undoubtedly neglect important factors.

Furthermore, insanity acquittal is a low base rate phenomenon.[107] Small sample sizes and low base rates limit one's ability to predict events. They also reduce the ability to generalize findings to other populations and settings. If a result can be obtained in varying settings and among varying populations, it is externally valid. Sound studies demand sufficient power to ensure that the results are not due to chance. The larger the sample size, the more likely one's results can be replicated in other settings with other populations.

Methodological Variation. In order to compare results across studies, a standardized method is useful. Once a finding has proven reliable across multiple researchers and settings, alternate methods can be employed in order to test the robustness of the particular finding. The methods used to measure criminal recidivism within the present studies, however, varied considerably without benefiting from an initial period of methodological consistency. The following four factors provided the most significant threats to the external validity of the findings.

i. Defining the Dependent Variable: The dependent variable was operationalized variably as police contacts, arrests, and convictions. This variation undoubtedly influenced the results. Convictions are a subset of arrests. In other words, not all people who are arrested are convicted. Therefore, arrest rates should always be higher than or equal to conviction rates. Similarly, police contact rates should always be higher than or equal to arrest rates. In some of the studies, the proportion of arrests that resulted in convictions was calculated.[108] If more studies obtained such proportions, a standardized "conversion rate" could be calculated. However, there is not enough data to integrate these results adequately. Therefore, the external validity of the results is limited.

ii. Data Collection Procedures: The means by which data were collected also varied considerably between studies. Criminal recidivism rates were obtained through conditional release committee records, official databases, police rap sheets, FBI records, corroborative reports by relatives, interviews with case workers and therapists, and self reports. The method by which the data were collected undoubtedly influenced the results obtained. Previous studies have established that self-reports of criminal activity among adults (adolescents often over-report) tend to produce deflated results.[109] Therefore, those studies using a self-report method would be expected to produce lower rates of recidivism. It is possible that other methods of data collection (e.g. corroborative reports by relatives) produce bias in the other direction. The variability among methods, and therefore shifting biases of the results, further limits the external validity of the findings.

iii. Length of follow up period: The length of follow up period ranged from 1 year[110] to as long as 17 years.[111] Therefore, it is little wonder that the rates of recidivism also varied from as low as 4.5%[112] to as high as 65.8%, 67.3%, and even 80.0%.[113] Preliminary efforts have been made to chart the change in recidivism rates over time;[114] however, more sophisticated modeling techniques are needed. It is clear that there is a strong linear relationship between length of follow up and re-arrest.[115] Furthermore, though acquittees appear to be most likely to recidivate within the first two years after discharge, there seems to be a troubling lack of a "ceiling effect" over time.[116] However, these conclusions are limited by the lack of adequate modeling studies. Until such techniques are applied to NGRI discharge patterns, it remains difficult to integrate results and therefore increase the external validity of the present findings.

iv. Inclusion Criteria: The majority of legislation on the insanity defense is created at the state level. Therefore, to be adjudicated NGRI in one state does not necessarily mean one has met the same criteria required in another state. For example, New York State adheres to the A.L.I standard (including cognitive and volitional components) whereas California adheres to the M'Naghten rule (including cognitive components solely). More restrictive criteria may select for more disturbed clients who are therefore more likely to be repeat offenders.

In a three state review by Weideranders and colleagues (1997), the researchers found that not only arrest rates but also other relevant factors varied by region (e.g. mean lengths of post-acquittal hospitalization). These regional differences appear to influence the research methods employed. For example, in Oregon and Missouri[117] less serious acquittees including misdemeanants have been studied. Whereas researchers in New York[118] have tended to focus on felony acquittees. Each of these sources of variation results in variable inclusion criteria and therefore limited external validity.

Internal Validity

A study is internally valid to the degree that the method can account fully for the results. In other words, if the method cannot rule out alternative explanations for a particular finding, the study lacks internal validity. Within the present review, variability in insanity defense success rates is the most salient threat to internal validity.

A primary focus of the NGRI criminal recidivism literature is to identify factors that distinguish recidivistic acquittees from non-recidivistic acquittees. As was discussed in an earlier section, the present review suggests that younger males with prior criminal histories appear to be most likely to be re-arrested after being released. However, research on the success rates of insanity defenses challenges the internal validity of these studies. A series of client characteristics have been associated with successful insanity defenses: female gender; age greater than 20 years old; unmarried; violent index crime other than murder; prior hospitalization; prior diagnosis of mental illness; and no prior criminal history.[119]

Using the gender results as an example, one can elucidate how these results threaten the internal validity of the NGRI recidivism studies. Females are more likely to be successful with an insanity defense.[120] The variation could be due to a variety of different factors: judges and juries may be biased toward females and therefore acquit less impaired females; females may be less likely to use the defense and therefore only use it when severely impaired; and/or insanity may become manifest in females in more clear and distinct patterns than males. The literature has not distinguished among these possibilities. If the first hypothesis were true, one would expect samples of female NGRI acquittees to include less serious cases with less potential to recidivate. Therefore, the suggestion within the present studies that males are more likely to recidivate may be due less to any quality within males than decision biases in judges and juries. Contradictory conclusions can be made if one assumes that the second hypothesis is true. Each of these hypotheses demands empirical study.

Releasing NGRI Acquittees into the Community
Two questions comprise the foundation of NGRI recidivism research: Who will recidivate and how is recidivism reduced? These two concerns, the prediction and prevention of NGRI criminal recidivism, shape both the research and policies affecting NGRI acquittees and their communities.

Predicting Criminal Recidivism
The twenty studies in this review suggest that younger males with prior criminal histories are most likely to recidivate. Beiber and colleagues (1988) attempted to use the available literature to predict which acquittees in a sample of 132 persons would be re-arrested. They found it easier to identify those who would not be re-arrested rather than those who would commit post-acquittal crimes. They were successful in 86.2% of the cases in predicting who would not recidivate, and only 52.6% of the cases in predicting who would recidivate. This attempt at predicting recidivism was conducted in 1988, however.

More sophisticated techniques for monitoring acquittees (e.g. survival analysis) are presently available.

Preventing Criminal Recidivism
Conditional release programs allow designated legal and mental health professionals to mandate outpatient treatment for acquittees released into the community. These monitored community treatments were developed primarily in the 1980s. In a review of such programs, Bloom and colleagues (1990) documented key legal decisions and legislative shifts that have facilitated their development. At the center of their review is the 1978 case *State v. Fields* in which the judges highlighted the competing concerns influencing the treatment of NGRI acquittees: the desire to provide the least restrictive treatment setting while protecting the community. These programs are an attempt to integrate these seemingly contradictory concerns.

The effectiveness of conditional release programs has been studied in a variety of geographic regions: NY, IL, CT, OH, CA, and OR. In a study that was not included in the present review because the sample included a small proportion of mentally disordered sex offenders, Wiederanders and colleagues (1992) followed 243 subjects who were grouped according to whether they were conditionally or unconditionally released into the community. The unconditionally released group was discharged because their commitment terms had expired. Therefore, it is possible they received outpatient treatment; however, such treatment was not mandated. The researchers found that 11 of the 190 conditionally released acquittees (5.8%) were re-arrested while 12 of the 44 unconditionally released acquittees (27.3%) recidivated. There were no statistically significant clinical or demographic differences between the groups. Therefore, the researchers concluded that the unconditionally released acquittees were more than four times as likely to be re-arrested.

The durability of such reductions has not been studied sufficiently however. Bloom and colleagues (1986) found that 31 of 132 acquittees (25.2%) were re-arrested while participating in Oregon's conditional release program. However, once the conditional release period expired and treatment was no longer mandated, 53 of the 123 acquittees (43.0%) were re-arrested. It is unclear whether a longer conditional release period would have produced more durable results.

Heilburn and Griffin (1993) reviewed twenty-two studies using data from conditional release programs. They examined the structure and recidivism data tied to these entities in order to identify the most salient characteristics of successful programs. They highlighted three principles. First, active communication must occur between the hospital staff, case managers, housing supervisors, service delivery agents, and review boards. Second, the balance between individual rights and protecting the community must be operationalized and monitored, and clearly articulated to the acquittee. Last, an empirical feedback system must be utilized in order to create a dynamic, evolving system.

For decades, criminal justice officials have attempted to use recidivism as a feedback process to analytical models that can be empirically validated.[121] These systems have evolved with developing statistical techniques. NGRI feedback systems need to have the capacity to adapt not only to new findings within the system itself and demographic shifts within the client pool, but also shifting legal codes. A system that is embedded within a particular legal stance can quickly become outdated given the rapidity with which insanity legislation is altered.[122]

Once a viable structure and information system is in place, the delivery of services at various stages in the release process can be studied. For example, Heilburn and colleagues (1994) assessed the influence of goodness of fit between released acquittees and their residences on subsequent functioning. Though their sample was not large enough to produce statistically significant results, they designed a model for studying the interaction between client and community residence characteristics.

The Psychiatric Security Review Board in Oregon has served as the template for many of these conditional release programs. It integrates criminal justice and mental health professionals with a research team. Within the context of such an integrative model, data collection, program design, and the delivery of services ideally occur simultaneously.[123] In a comparison across three states, Weideranders and colleagues (1997) found that the Oregon Psychiatric Review Board outperformed the other programs in terms of low recidivism rates and rapid return of acquittees to the community. Harris (2000) argued, however, that a transposition error significantly influenced the results and the Oregon program actually had the highest recidivism rates. She suggests that the shorter lengths of hospitalization may be casually related to the increased recidivism.

The discrepancy points to a central issue in the literature: the relationship between re-arrest and re-hospitalization. Numerous researchers have argued that re-hospitalization is a proper means for preventing criminal recidivism.[124] One of the primary strengths of psychiatric review boards is the efficient revocation of releases. If a person appears to be decompensating, trained personnel can swiftly re-hospitalize the person without having to pass through the normal bureaucratic pathways. Within an effective conditional release program, acquittees' symptoms are monitored regularly in order to intervene before escalating problems place both the acquittee and the community in danger.

In one of the most sophisticated studies in the literature, Wiederanders (1992) calculated survival analyses of NGRI acquittees (and mentally disordered sex offenders) who had been conditionally and unconditionally released into the community. By calculating survival analyses, he accounted for temporary revocations, hospitalizations and other factors that influenced the time at risk for the subjects. In an initial analysis of criminal recidivism, he found that conditionally released subjects were in the community significantly longer before being re-arrested than the unconditionally released group. However, once he included hospitalization data as a factor affecting time at risk, he found that the two groups had comparable re-arrest data. He concluded that the revocation of a conditional release through re-hospitalization prevented acquittees from committing subsequent offenses. It is possible that the events that led to revocation would have led to arrest had the acquittee not been in the conditional release program. In other words, it may be that conditionally and unconditionally released acquittees are committing comparable acts but simply being tracked along different pathways. However, Wiederanders concludes that hospitalization most likely serves some type of preventive function.

Wiederanders also highlights the cost savings in conditional release programs. A common assumption in the literature is that conditionally released acquittees are released into the community faster and therefore spend less time in the hospital than unconditionally released persons. Therefore cost comparisons between hospitalization and conditional release programs are typically made. Within California, the cost per-client within the conditional release program is one-fifth the cost of holding an individual for a comparable period of time in the state hospital.

Bigelow and colleagues (1990) found that monitored community treatments cost 14% of the hospitalization costs they replace.[125] Furthermore, community treatment of NGRI acquittees frees limited beds within the state hospitals. In certain jurisdictions in Missouri, insanity acquittees occupy the majority of long-term psychiatric hospital beds.[126] Given that conditional release programs seem to be successful in reducing recidivism and have become increasingly utilized during the past two decades, one would expect rates of recidivism to decrease over time. It is difficult to assess overall trends given the differences between studies mentioned previously. Also, other trends that would lead to the inflation of recidivism rates may counter the influence of conditional release programs. For example, the shift toward community mental health care and therefore reduced hospitalization stays may lead to more recidivism. Similarly, broader population changes in crime rates would affect NGRI recidivism. These are empirical issues that demand further study.

Incorporating Hospital Recidivism Data

Wiederanders' suggestion (1992) that hospital and criminal recidivism are dynamically related has been frequently cited but rarely studied. Tables 7 through 10 summarize the NGRI hospital recidivism literature in a manner paralleling the previous review of criminal recidivism studies. Hospital recidivism results, like criminal recidivism findings, vary considerably across regions and time periods. In comparing Tables 1 and 7, there appears to be no consistent relationship between re-arrest and re-hospitalization. Wiederanders' suggestion that hospitalization may serve a preventive function in reducing re-arrest demands direct empirical study.

Table 7: Studies in NGRI hospital recidivism

Study	Site	N	Follow-Up	Re-Hospitalizations	Correlates
Morrow et al., 1966	MO	35	< 6 yrs	8/35 22.9%	NA
Pasewark et al., 1979	NY	107	< 11.2 yrs	23/107 21.5% μ=0.44	Female
Pantle et al., 1980	NY	37	5.5–11.5 yrs	4/37 10.8% μ=0.27	Female
Pasewark et al., 1982	NY	33	3–6 yrs	6/33 18.2% μ=0.58	Female
Pasewark et al., 1982	NY	107	5–10 yrs	23/107 21.5% μ=0.44	NA
Rogers et al., 1982	OR	165	< 3 yrs	NA	NA
Rogers et al., 1984	OR	295	1.2–5.1 yrs	NA	NA
Spodak et al., 1984	MD	86	5–15 yrs μ=9.5	NA	NA

Table continues

Table 7: Studies in NGRI hospital recidivism -- continued

Study	Site	N	Follow-Up	Re-Hospitalizations	Correlates
Cavanaugh et al., 1985	IL	44	1–2 yrs	11/44 25.0%	Substance use, Medication noncompliance
Bloom et al., 1986	OR	123	< 3 yrs	NA	NA
Bloom et al., 1986	OR	67	2 yrs	28/67 41.8%	NA
Bogenberger et al., 1987	HI	107	8–14.5 yrs	44/107 $\mu=0.98$ 41.1%	Males
Beiber et al., 1988	NY	132	5–10 yrs	NA	NA
Lamb et al., 1988	CA	79	3.8 yrs	37/79 46.8%	No mandated outpatient treatment
Silver et al., 1989	MD	127	7–17 yrs $\mu=10$	58/127 $\mu=1.4$ 45.7%	MI non-offenders > NGRI > offenders

Table continues

Table 7: Studies in NGRI hospital recidivism -- continued

Study	Site	N	Follow-Up		Re-Hospitalizations		Correlates
Nicholson et al, 1991	OK	30	2.75 yrs	μ=3.0	10/30	33.3%	Treated=Released=AWOL
McGreevy et al., 1991	NY	331	3.8 yrs		93–166/331	28.0-50.2%	NA
Stafford et al., 1997	OH	38	NA		13/38	34.2%	NA
Luettgen et al., 1998	CAN	74	6.7 yrs	μ=2.6	64/74	92.4%	Substance use
Kravitz et al., 1999	IL	36	4.9–18.4 yrs	μ=1.9	20/36	55.6%	NA

Table 8: Range of NGRI hospital recidivism rates

Range	Study	Result
Maximum	Luettgen et al., 1998	92.4%
Minimum	Pantle et al., 1980	10.8%

Table 9: Correlates of hospital recidivism

Correlates of Recidivism	Studies
Female	Pasewark et al., 1979; Pantle et al., 1980; Pasewark et al, 1982
Substance Abuse	Cavanaugh et al., 1985; Luettgen et al., 1998
Medication Non-Compliance	Cavanaugh et al., 1985
No Mandated Outpatient Treatment	Lamb et al., 1988
Male	Bogenberger et al., 1986

Table 10: Group comparisons of hospital recidivism rates

Study	Result
Silver et al., 1989	Mentally ill non-offenders > NGRI > Offenders
Nicholson et al., 1991	Treated NGRI = Untreated NGRI = AWOL

Study Description

The present study is a retrospective chart review, following seventy-three NGRI acquittees within a major metropolitan area between six and eighteen years. It will serve six salient purposes. First, it will expand our understanding of the clinical characteristics of NGRI acquittees by incorporating broader caregiver and community factors (e.g. caregiver involvement and safety of home environment). Second, it will provide an extended and detailed description of the criminal and hospital recidivism patterns of a group of NGRI acquittees within a major metropolitan region. Third, it will identify unique clinical and demographic factors that predict criminal and hospital recidivism and build logistic regression models that will account for maximal variability using the simplest procedures. Forth, it will assess the clinical progress of the acquittees from admission to discharge during the NGRI hospital stay. Fifth, it will examine the relationship between criminal and hospital recidivism in order to determine whether hospital admission serves a preventive function in reducing re-arrest. Last, it will compare veteran to non-veteran NGRI acquittees in order to determine whether the veterans comprise a unique clinical group.

[41]Lymburner, J. A., & Roesch, R. (1999). The insanity defense: Five years of research, 1993-1997. (1999). *International Journal of Psychiatry and Law*, 22(3-4), 213-240; Harris, V. L. (2000). Insanity acquittees and rearrest: The past 24 years. *Journal of American Academy of Psychiatry and Law*, 28, 225-231.

[42]Steadman, H. J., & Keveles, G. (1972). The community adjustment and criminal activity of the Baxstrom patients: 1966-1970. *American Journal of Psychiatry*, 129(3), 80-86; Vartianinen, H., & Hakola, P. (1992). Monitored conditional release of persons found not guilty by reason of insanity. *American Journal of Psychiatry*, 149(3), 415; Wiederanders, M. R. (1992). Recidivism of disordered offenders who were conditionally vs. unconditionally released. *Behavioral Sciences and the Law*, 10, 141-148; Zeidler, J. C., Haines, W. H., Tikuisis, V., & Uffelman, E. J. (1955). A follow-up study of patients discharged from a hospital for the criminally insane. *Journal of Social Therapy*, 1(2), 21-24; Wiederanders, M. R., & Choate, P. A. (1994). Beyond recidivism: Measuring community adjustments of conditionally released insanity acquittees. *Psychological Assessment*, 6(1), 61-66; Harris, V., & Koepsell, T. D. (1996). Criminal recidivism in mentally ill offenders: A pilot study. Bulletin of the American Academy of Psychiatry and Law, 24(2), 177-186.

[43]Steadman; Wiederanders, 1992; Harris.

[44]Wiederanders & Choate.

[45]Vartiainen.

[46]Sreenivasan, S., Kirkish, P., Shoptaw, S., Welsh, R. K., & Ling, W. (2000). Neuropsychological and diagnostic differences between recidivistically violent not criminally responsible and mentally ill prisoners. *International Journal of Law and Psychiatry*, 23(2), 161-172.

[47]Pasewark, R. A., Pantle, M. L., & Steadman, H. J. (1982). Detention and rearrest rates of persons found not guilty by reason of insanity and convicted felons. *American Journal of Psychiatry*, 139(7), 892-897.

[48]McGreevy, M. A., Steadman, H. J., Dvoskin, J. A., & Dollard, N. (1991). New York State's system of managing insanity acquittees in the community. *Hospital and Community Psychiatry*, 42(5), 512-517.

[49]Callahan, L. A., & Silver, E. (1998). Factors associated with the conditional release of persons acquitted by reason of insanity: A decision tree approach. *Law and Human Behavior*, 22(2), 151.

[50]Pasewark, Pantle, & Steadman, 1982.

[51]Pasewark, Pantle, & Steadman, 1979.

[52]Pasewark et al., 1979. Pantle et al., 1980. Pasewark et al., 1982.

[53]Harris, 2000.

[54]Morrow, W. R., & Peterson, D. B. (1966). Follow-up of discharged psychiatric offenders: Not guilty by reason of insanity and criminal sexual psychopaths. *Journal of Criminal Law, Criminology and Police Science*, 57(1), 31-34; Bloom et al., 1986; Luettgen et al., 1998.

[55]Luettgen.

[56]Bloom et al., 1986. Luettgen, 1998.

[57]Beiber et al., 1988. Luettgen et al., 1998.

[58]Luettgen.

[59]Kravitz, H. M., & Kelly, J. (1999). An outpatient psychiatry program for offenders with mental disorders found not guilty by reason of insanity. *Psychiatric Services*, 50(12), 1597-1605.

[60]Pantle. Pasewark, 1982.

[61]Silver.

[62]Ibid

[63]Morrow & Peterson, 1966; Luettgen et al., 1988.

[64]Lymburner & Roesch, 1999; Cirincione, C., Steadman, H. J., & McGreevy, M. A. (1995). Rates of insanity acquittals and the factors associated with successful insanity pleas. *Bulletin of the American Academy of Psychiatry and Law*, 23(3), 399-409.

[65]United States Department of Justice: Prison and jail inmates at midyear 2002. *Bureau of Justice Statistics*, NJC 198877, April 2003.

[66]Lymburner & Roesch, 1999.

[67]Ibid; Bloom & Williams, 1994; Cirincione et al., 1995; Roesch et al., 1997.

[68]Morrow & Peterson, 1966; Silver et al., 1989.

[69]Cavanaugh & Wasyliw, 1985. Treating the not guilty by reason of insanity outpatient: A two-year study. *Bulletin of the American Academy of Psychiatry and Law*, 13(4), 407-415.

[70]Douglas, K. S., Ogloff, J. R., Nicholls, T. L., & Grant, I. (1999). Assessing risk for violence among psychiatric patients: The HCR-20 violence risk assessment scheme and the psychopathy checklist: Screening version. *Journal of Consulting Psychology*, 67(6), 917-930; Harris, 2000.

[71]Pasewark et al., 1979; Pasewark et al., 1980; Pasewark et al., 1982; Luettgen et al., 1998.

[72]Bloom et al., 1986.

[73]Pasewark et al., 1979; Pasewark et al., 1982.

[74]Cirincione & Jacobs, 1999.

[75]Douglas et al., 1999; Harris, 2000.

[76]Steadman, 1985.

[77]Phillips, B. L., & Pasewark, R. A. (1980). Insanity plea in Connecticut. *Bulletin of the American Academy of Psychiatry and Law*, 3(3), 335-344.

[78]Cirincione et al., 1995.

[79]Cavanaugh & Wasyliw, 1985.

[80]Morrow & Peterson, 1966.

[81]Bogenberger et al., 1987.

[82]Lamb, H. R., Weinberger, L. E., & Gross, B. H. (1988). Court-mandated community outpatient treatment for persons found not guilty by reason of insanity: A five-year follow-up. *American Journal of Psychiatry*, 145(4), 450-456.

[83]Cavanaugh & Wasyliw, 1985.

[84]Cirincione, Steadman, & McGreevy, 1995.

[85]Lymburner & Roesch; Cirincione et al.

[86]Phillips, & Pasewark (1980).

[87]Morrow & Peterson, 1966.

[88]Kravitz, & Kelly, 1999.

[89]Cirincione, C., Steadman, H. J., & McGreevy, M. A. (1995).

[90]Nicholson, R. A., Norwood, S., & Enyart, C. (1991). Characteristics and outcomes of insanity acquittees in Oklahoma. *Behavioral Sciences and the Law*, 9, 487-500.

[91]Kravitz, & Kelly, 1999.

[92]Bieber, S. L., Pasewark, R. A., Bosten, K., & Steadman, H. J. (1988). *International Journal of Law and Psychiatry*, 11, 105-112.

[93]Bogenberger, Pasewark, Gudeman, & Beiber, 1987.

[94]Harris, V. L. (2000).

[95]Douglas, Ogloff, Nicholls, & Grant, 1999.

[96]Lymburner, & Roesch, 1999.

[97]Wack, 1993; Roesch et al., 1997; Cirincoine et al., 1995.

[98]Lymburner, & Roesch.

[99]Cavanaugh & Wasyliw, 1985.

[100]Lamb et al., 1988.

[101]Sreenivasan et al., 2000; Abram & Teplin, 1999; Swanson et al., 1990.

[102]Gutheil, 1999.

[103]Ibid.

[104]Perlin, 1996; Rogers et al., 1984; Fukanaga, K. K., Pasewark, R. A., Hawkins, M., & Gudeman, H. (1981). Insanity plea: Interexaminer agreement and concordance of psychiatric opinion and court verdict. *Law and Human Behavior*, 5(4), 325-328.

[105]Clark, C. R., Holden, C. E., Thompson, J. S., Watson, P. L., & Wightman, L. H. (1993). Forensic treatment in the United States: A survey of selected forensic hospitals. Treatment at Michigan's Forensic Center. *International Journal of Law and Psychiatry*, 16(1-2), 71-81; Silver, E. (1995). Punishment or treatment? Comparing the lengths of confinement of successful and unsuccessful insanity defendants. *Law and Human Behavior*, 19(4), 375-388.

[106]Bloom et al., 1990.

[107]Kravitz et al., 1999.

[108]Spodak, M. K., Silver, S. B., & Wright, C. U. (1984). Criminality of discharged insanity acquittees: Fifteen year experience in Maryland reviewed. *Bulletin of the American Academy of Psychiatry and* Law, 12(4), 373-383.

[109]Gottfredson, M. R., & Hirschi, T. (1990). *A general theory of crime.* Stanford: Stanford University Press.

[110]Cavanuagh & Wasyliw, 1985.

[111]Silver et al., 1989.

[112]Cavanuagh.

[113]Silver et al., 1989; Bogenberger et al., 1987; Nicholson et al., 1991.

[114]Silver et al., 1989.

[115]Harris, 2000.

[116]Ibid.

[117]Bloom et al., 1986; Petrila, J. (1982). The insanity defense and other mental health dispositions in Missouri. *International Journal of Law and Psychiatry*, 5(1), 81-101.

[118]Steadman, 1980.

[119]Cirincione et al., 1995.

[120]Ibid

[121]Belkin, J., Blumstein, A., & Glass, W. (1973). Recidivism as a feedback process: An analytical model and empirical validation. *Journal of Criminal Justice*, 1, 7-26.

[122]Heilbrun, K., & Griffin, P. A. (1993). Community-based forensic treatment of insanity acquittees. *International Journal of Law and Psychiatry*, 16, 133-150.

[123]Bloom, J. D., & Williams, M. H. (1994). *Management and treatment of insanity Acquittees: A model for the 1990s*. Washington D.C.: American Psychiatric Press.

[124]Wiederanders, 1992.

[125]Heilbrun & Griffin, 1993.

[126]Linhorst & Dirks-Linhorst, 1997; Lymburner, 1999.

CHAPTER 3
Conducting a Study

Sample
The sample for the present study is comprised of all NGRI acquittees conditionally released in Cook County, Illinois, between January 1, 1983 and December 31, 1995. Cook County encompasses the metropolitan area surrounding and including Chicago, Illinois.

Procedure
The Illinois Department of Human Services' Office of Mental Health (IOMH) compiled an exhaustive list of NGRI acquittees released in Cook County during the study time period. Even though the most violent acquittees were often treated in a facility outside of the county, they were assessed at Elgin State Mental Health Center at admission and then returned to Elgin before being released into the community.

Identification codes unique to this project were assigned to each of the 93 acquittees so that the demographic, arrest and hospitalization data could be separated from the personal identifying information. First the hospitalization data were collected. OMH staff compiled hospitalization logs for each of the acquittees using the Department of Human Service's electronic database. These logs were given to the researcher, thereby allowing him to document the acquittees' admission and discharge dates from state psychiatric facilities before and after the index crime.

Second the arrest data were collected in the following manner. The list of acquittees was sent to the Cook County Public Defender's Office. Staff supplied the researcher with arrest dates, charges and dispositions for each pre-NGRI, NGRI and post-NGRI arrest.

The list was also sent to Elgin State Mental Health Center--the facility that houses the records for NGRI acquittees who are conditionally released into the community. Staff members assembled the complete records for those acquittees for whom they still had documentation. The researcher then conducted on-site, retrospective chart reviews for each individual. The chart reviews allowed the researcher to collect demographic information, DSM-IV diagnoses, and admission and discharge dates for private hospitals, and assess the clinical functioning of the acquittees at admission and discharge from Elgin State Mental Health Center. Clinical functioning was evaluated using the Adult Needs and Strengths Assessment instrument (ANSA) that will be described in the measures section.

Of the 93 acquittees on the list, Elgin had complete records for 73 individuals. Seven acquittees' records had been sent to other psychiatric facilities and thirteen records could not be located. The medical records department was being re-located due to budgetary constraints during the period of the study. The move most likely exacerbated difficulties locating the additional thirteen records. Comparisons were conducted, using the hospitalization and arrest data, in order to determine whether there were any significant differences between the acquittees whose records could be located and those records not included in the study. The only significant difference was that the acquittees whose records could not be located experienced significantly more post-index-crime hospitalizations (M = 1.00, S.D. = 0.97, p < 0.01) than the group for whom the ANSA data could be collected (M = 0.18, S.D. = 0.48). This finding is reasonable given that the acquittees who experienced more hospitalizations would be more likely to have their records shipped to other facilities.

Measures

The Adult Needs and Strengths Assessment instrument (ANSA) was used in conducting the chart reviews. The ANSA is a modified version of the Severity of Psychiatric Illness (SPI) instrument.[127] It not only measures the same client and caregiver vulnerabilities measured in the SPI (e.g. psychosis and depression/anxiety), but also assesses client and caregiver strengths (e.g. spirituality/religious and talents/interests). Appendix B includes the items used in this study as outlined in the ANSA manual.

The SPI is a reliable and valid measure of psychiatric and social characteristics related to decisions about level of care, service use, and outcomes monitoring.[128] It can be used either as a retrospective chart review tool with reliability above 0.80 or as a prospective decision support, outcomes management tool. Even when used retrospectively, it has been validly related to independent, directed, structured assessment measures such as the BPRS.[129] When used in planning studies, it measures factors thought to enable service delivery systems to address the needs of persons with psychiatric disturbances better.[130]

The ANSA uses a four-point rating scale structured to inform clinical decision-making and guide clinical interventions. Each item includes the following scale: '0' implies no need for action given the lack of available evidence; '1' suggests the need for ongoing monitoring and potential preventive interventions given prior symptoms and/or the likelihood of future problematic developments; '2' suggests the presence of moderate psychiatric disturbance that demands direct intervention; and '3' implies immediate and extensive action is necessary given the severity of the symptoms.[131]   Once a person demonstrates elevations above a '1,' some degree of clinical treatment will most likely be necessary.

The present researcher conducted all of the chart reviews. In order to assess inter-rater reliability, he scored two random profiles that were reviewed by the ANSA's developer, Dr. John S. Lyons. The inter-rater agreement was 0.87 and 0.89.

Statistical Analyses

Independent t-tests were conducted in order to compare groups (e.g. recidivates vs. non-recidivates; acquittees at admission vs. acquittees at discharge; and veterans vs. non-veterans) according to a variety of demographic, clinical functioning, and recidivism variables.

Odds ratios and percent differences were calculated for each ANSA item's relation to re-arrest and re-hospitalization. Odds ratios not only demonstrate relative differences but also quantify the extent of the differences.

Stepwise logistic regression models, constructed through a forward entry conditional approach, systemized the prediction of re-arrest and re-hospitalization. Each predictor is entered separately and is considered linear with respect to log odds. These models allowed for maximal accounting for variance within the dependent variables while limiting overlap among predictors.

Survival analyses were not conducted on the sample of acquittees given the inability to account for time at risk reliably. There were too many gaps in the Public Defender's database, making it impossible to determine precisely when acquittees entered and left the prison system. More reliable data could have been collected if rap sheets were reviewed and criminal case histories had been studied in greater depth. Such procedures would have demanded additional levels of access that were not gained during the study period.

---

[127]Lyons, J. S., Colletta, J., Devens, M., & Finkel, S.I. (1995). The validity of the Severity of Psychiatric Illness in a sample of inpatients in a psychogeriatrics unit, *International Psychogeriatrics*, 7, 407-416.

[128]Lyons, J. S., Stutesman, J., Neme, J., Vessey, J. T., O'Mahoney, M. T., & Camper, H. J. (1997). Predicting readmissions to the psychiatric emergency admissions and hospital outcomes. *Medical Care*, 35, 792-800.

[129]Lyons, et al, 1995.

[130]Anderson, R. L., & Lyons, J. S. (2001). Needs-based planning for persons with serious mental illness residing in intermediate care facilities. *Journal of Behavioral Health Services Research*, 28(1), 104-110.

[131]Lyons, 1995.

CHAPTER 4

Findings from the Study

Descriptive Statistics
Sample Demographics
Table 11 describes the demographic statistics of the sample (N = 73) at the time of the index offense. The acquittees were predominantly male (N = 54, 74.0%), African-American (N = 43, 58.9%), and born within Cook County (N = 49, 67.1%). They tended neither to have been married (N = 34, 46.6%), nor served in the military (N = 63, 86.3%), and the majority were not employed at the time of the index offense (N = 41, 56.2%). The mean age was approximately 40 years old (SD = 12.95).

Tracking
The follow-up period ended July 1, 2002. As described in Table 12, the mean follow-up period was 8.68 years (SD = 624.91), and the range spanned from 6.44 to 17.21 years. There was considerable variation concerning the lengths of the NGRI hospital stays. The mean stay was 3.85 years (SD = 4.10). However, the results ranged from 34 days to 13.48 years.

Table 11: Demographic statistics

Characteristic	N (Total = 73)	%	Mean	S.D.
Age	--	--	40.44	12.95
Children	44	60.3%	1.34	1.47
Gender				
Female	19	26.0%	--	--
Male	54	74.0%	--	--
Marital Status				
Divorced	23	31.5%	--	--
Married	6	8.2%	--	--
Single	34	46.6%	--	--
Other	10	13.7%	--	--
Occupation				
Employed	24	32.9%	--	--
Unemployed	41	56.2	--	--
Other	8	11.0%	--	--
Race				
Caucasian	27	37.0%	--	--
Afr-American	43	58.9%	--	--
Other	3	4.1%	--	--
Veteran Status	10	13.7%	--	--

Table 12: Utilization data

Variable	Minimum	Maximum	Mean	SD
Length of NGRI Stay (days)	34	4920	1404.55	1497.61
Follow-up Period (years)	6.44	17.21	8.68	1.71

Pre-Index Crime Arrest and Hospitalization Data

Table 13 describes the pre-index crime arrest data. The majority of acquittees had been arrested prior to the index crime (N = 41, 56.2%), and a substantial group had been arrested previously for violent crimes (N = 25, 34.2%). The list of crimes considered violent is outlined in Table 14. Of those who had been previously arrested, the mean number of arrests was 2.33 (SD = 4.18). Of those who had previously been arrested for violent crimes, the mean number of arrests for any type of crime was 0.67 (SD = 1.19). The violent offenders committed more severe but less frequent criminal acts.

Table 13: Pre-index crime criminal justice statistics

Characteristic	N (Total = 73)	%	Mean	S.D.
Prior Arrest	41	56.2%	2.33	4.18
Prior Arrest for Violent Crime	25	34.2%	0.67	1.19

Table 14: List of crimes acquittees committed deemed violent

Crime

Aggravated arson
Aggravated assault
Aggravated battery
Aggravated robbery
Aggravated criminal sexual assault
Armed violence
Assault
Attempted murder
Battery
Criminal sexual assault
Cruelty to children
Deviant sexual assault
Kidnapping
Murder
Manslaughter
Rape
Unlawful restraint

Table 15 describes the pre-index crime hospitalization data. The majority of acquittees had been hospitalized prior to the index offense (N = 51, 70.0%). Twenty-two acquittees (30.1%) had never been hospitalized; seventeen (23.3.%) had been hospitalized once; and thirty-four acquittees (46.6%) had been hospitalized at least two times prior to the index offense.

Table 15: Pre-index crime hospitalization statistics

Characteristic	N (Total = 73)	%
Prior hospitalizations		
None	22	30.1%
One	17	23.3%
At Least Two	34	46.6%

Index Crime Arrest and Hospitalization Data

Tables 16 and 17 describe the index crime charges and NGRI diagnoses, respectively. The most frequent index crime charge was murder (N = 35, 47.9%). Arson (N = 9, 12.3%), Battery (N = 9, 12.3%), and Burglary (N = 8, 11.0%) were also common among the study sample. The additional charges (e.g. Armed Violence, Assault, Car Jacking, Forgery, Home Invasion, Involuntary Manslaughter, Possession of a Controlled Substance, Sexual Assault, Theft, and Weapons Possession) were committed by two or less acquittees ($\leq 2.7\%$).

Table 16: Index crime charges

Charge	N (Total = 73)	%
Murder	35	47.9%
Arson	9	12.3%
Battery	9	12.3%
Burglary	8	11.0%
Robbery	2	2.7%
Armed Violence	1	1.4%
Assault	1	1.4%
Carjacking	1	1.4%
Forgery	1	1.4%
Home Invasion	1	1.4%
Involuntary Manslaughter	1	1.4%
Possession of a Controlled Subs.	1	1.4%
Sexual Assault	1	1.4%
Theft	1	1.4%
Weapons	1	1.4%

Table 17: NGRI index diagnoses

Diagnosis*	N (Total = 73)	%
Substance Use Disorder	52	71.2%
Psychotic Disorder	39	53.4%
Mood Disorder	30	41.1%
Personality Disorder	26	35.6%
Anxiety Disorder	1	1.4%

*Multiple diagnoses possible per individual.

NGRI diagnoses were counted by type and not by case; therefore, given that many acquittees had comorbid disorders, the sum of the disorders (N = 148) more than doubles the total number of acquittees (N = 73). The majority of individuals were diagnosed with substance use disorders (N = 52, 71.2%) and/or psychotic disorders (N = 39, 53.4%) at the time of their index hospitalization. Mood disorders (N = 30, 41.1%) and personality disorders (N = 26, 35.6%) were also quite common.

Recidivism Data

Tables 18 summarizes the criminal recidivism data for the sample. Of the seventy-three acquittees, twenty-three (31.5%) were re-arrested. These re-offenders averaged 3.43 arrests per person (SD = 3.04). Only 12 acquittees (16.4%) were re-arrested for violent crimes. Of all acquittees who were re-arrested, five individuals (21.7%) recidivated within the first year of their conditional release. More than sixty percent of the recidivates (14 acquittees) experienced their first post-release arrest between one and five years. The remaining four acquittees (17.4%) were not arrested until after five years post-release (see Figure 1).

When counting not only first arrests, but all arrests, a similar pattern emerges. Eight arrests (10.1%) occurred within the first year, 43 arrests (54.4%) between one and five years, 24 arrests (30.4%) between five and ten years, and four arrests (5.1%) occurred after ten years. Not all individuals were followed for more than ten years however.

Table 18: Criminal recidivism data

Variable	Ratio	Percent	Mean	SD
Acquittees Re-Arrested	23	31.5%	3.43*	3.04
Acquittees Re-Arrested for a Violent Crime	12	16.4%	--	--
Total Number of Re-Arrests	80	--	--	--
Total Number Violent Re-Arrests	19	23.8%	--	--
Total Number of Domestic Battery Charges	12	63.2%**	--	--
Time Span of First Post-Release Arrests				
< 1 year	5	21.7%	--	--
1 – 5 years	14	60.9%	--	--
5 – 10 years	4	17.4%	--	--
> 10 years	0	0.0%	--	--
Time Span of All Post-Release Arrests				
< 1 year	8	10.1%	--	--
1 – 5 years	43	54.4%	--	--
5 – 10 years	24	30.4%	--	--
> 10 years	4	5.1%	--	--

*Mean number of re-arrests for those acquittees who were re-arrested
**Percentage of domestic abuse charges out of the total number of re-arrests for violent crimes

Figure 1: Proportion of subjects re-arrested over time

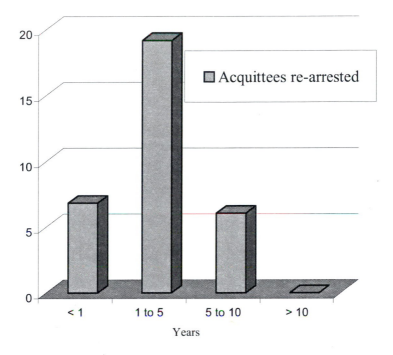

Table 19 summarizes the hospital recidivism patterns for the sample. Eleven acquittees (15.1%) were re-hospitalized during the follow-up period. Of the recidivates, the mean number of hospitalizations was 1.27 (SD = 0.47). The hospital recidivates tended to experience their first post-release hospitalizations between one and five years after discharge (N = 8, 72.7%). Only three recidivates (27.3%) were re-hospitalized within the first year and no acquittees experienced their first post-release hospitalization after five years (see Figure 2).

Table 19: Hospital recidivism data

Variable	Ratio	Percent	Mean	SD
Acquittees Re-Hospitalized	11	15.1%	1.27	0.47
Time Span of First Post-Release Hospitalizations				
< 1 year	3	27.3%	--	--
1 – 5 years	8	72.7%	--	--
5 – 10 years	0	0.0%	--	--
> 10 years	0	0.0%	--	--
Time Span of All Post-Release Hospitalizations				
< 1 year	3	21.4%	--	--
1 – 5 years	9	64.3%	--	--
5 – 10 years	1	7.1%	--	--
> 10 years	0	0.0%	--	--

Figure 2: Proportion of subjects re-hospitalized over time

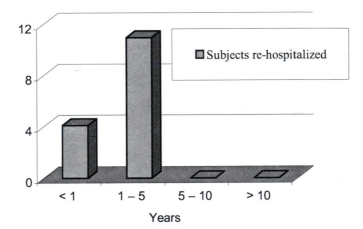

80

When accounting not only for first clinical relapses but also subsequent hospitalizations, the previously described pattern is reinforced. The majority of recidivates were re-hospitalized between one and five years post-discharge (N = 9, 64.3%); whereas, a smaller group was hospitalized within the first year (N = 3, 21.4%) and one acquittee was hospitalized between five and ten years (7.1%).

Chart Review Data
ANSA Scores at Admission
The ANSA item scores for the acquittees at the index admission are listed in Table 20. In terms of the Problem Presentation subset, the acquittees demonstrated frequent and severe psychotic symptoms (Mean = 2.45, SD = 0.58) and appeared to be using large amounts of chemical substances (Mean = 2.01, SD 1.16). They demonstrated moderate levels of depressive and anxious symptoms (Mean = 1.99, 0.59), antisocial tendencies (Mean = 1.34, SD 0.85), and broad patterns of personality disturbance (Mean = 1.16, SD = 0.88).

Each of the items within the Problem Modifiers subset suggested the need for intervention. The acquittees' symptoms tended to be consistent across situations (Mean = 2.60, SD 0.49) and over time (Mean = 2.10, SD = 0.34); and the acquittees tended to have little motivation for treatment (Mean = 1.96, SD = 0.48). In terms of risk behaviors, they appeared dangerous both to self (Mean = 1.85, SD = 0.83) and others (Mean = 2.44, 0.73), tended to engage in criminal activity (Mean = 2.64, SD = 0.51), and demonstrated somewhat problematic social patterns (Mean = 1.75, SD = 0.49).

The Functioning subset revealed varying degrees of impairment. The acquittees tended to know little about their illnesses (Mean = 2.01, SD = 0.46) and function poorly both at work and school (Mean = 1.82, SD = 0.48). In addition, they appeared to have had moderate impairments in family functioning (Mean = 1.30, SD = 0.66), independent living skills (Mean = 1.29, SD = 0.75), and residential stability (Mean = 1.25, SD = 0.68) either in the past or would most likely experience such difficulties in the future.

In terms of the intensity of care each acquittee needed, all items were elevated. The acquittees tended to be poorly organized (Mean = 2.18, SD = 0.48), have limited resources (Mean = 1.77, SD = 0.54), and necessitate intense and consistent monitoring (Mean = 2.16, SD = 0.50). Most acquittees resisted taking psychotropic medications (Mean = 2.10, SD = 0.56), had difficulties caring for themselves (Mean = 1.49, SD = 0.67), and had transient relationships with clinicians (Mean = 1.60, SD = 0.66).

Table 20: Adult Needs and Strengths Assessment scores
at NGRI admission

Category	Item	Minimum	Maximum	Mean	S.D.
Problem Presentation					
	Psychosis	1	3	2.45	0.58
	Impulsivity	0	3	0.96	0.92
	Depress./Anx.	1	3	1.99	0.59
	Antisocial	0	3	1.34	0.85
	Substance Abuse	0	3	2.01	1.16
	Adj. to Trauma	0	2	0.67	0.77
	Personality Dis.	0	3	1.16	0.88
Problem Modifiers					
	Situational. Consistency	2	3	2.60	0.49
	Temporal Consistency	1	3	2.10	0.34
	Motivation for Treatment	1	3	1.96	0.48
Risk Behaviors					
	Danger to Self	0	3	1.85	0.83
	Danger to Other	0	3	2.44	0.73
	Sex. Inappropr.	0	2	0.36	0.67
	Social Behavior	0	3	1.75	0.49
	Crime	1	3	2.64	0.51
	Victimization	0	3	0.67	0.91

Table Continues

Table 20: Adult Needs and Strengths Assessment scores
at NGRI admission -- Continued

Category	Item	Minimum	Maximum	Mean	S.D.
Problem Presentation					
	Intellect. Funct.	0	3	0.60	0.68
	Knowledge Of Illness	1	3	2.01	0.46
	Physical/Medical	0	2	0.96	0.86
	Family Function.	0	2	1.30	0.66
	Employment/ Education	1	3	1.82	0.48
	Independent Living Skills	0	3	1.29	0.75
	Resident. Stability	0	3	1.25	0.68
Care Intensity and Organization					
	Resources	0	3	1.77	0.54
	Organization	1	3	2.18	0.48
	Monitoring	1	3	2.16	0.50
	Treatment Intensity	1	3	2.22	0.45
	Service Permanence	0	3	1.60	0.66
	Self-Care	0	2	1.49	0.67
	Medical Complications	1	3	2.10	0.56
Family/Caregiver Capacities					
	Caregiver Health	0	3	1.19	0.83
	Caregiver Involvement	0	3	1.58	0.64
	Caregiver Knowledge	1	3	1.78	0.48
	Caregiver Safety	0	3	0.63	0.72

Table Continues

84

Table 20: Adult Needs and Strengths Assessment scores
at NGRI admission -- Continued

Category	Item	Minimum	Maximum	Mean	S.D.
Strengths					
	Family	1	3	2.67	0.55
	Interpersonal Skills	1	3	2.55	0.55
	Relationship Permanence	1	3	2.71	0.49
	Vocational	1	3	2.67	0.50
	Spirituality/ Religious	1	3	2.81	0.50
	Talents/Interests	1	3	2.63	0.54
	Inclusion in the Community	2	3	2.86	0.35

Relatives, close friends, and intimate partners who were directly involved in caring for the acquittees were considered to be caregivers. The acquittees' caregivers demonstrated limited knowledge of the acquittees' illnesses (Mean = 1.78, SD = 0.48) and modest involvement in their treatments (Mean = 1.58, SD = 0.64). The caregiving environments, however, tended to be relatively safe (Mean = 0.63, SD = 0.72).

Within the Strengths subset, the acquittees demonstrated limited protective factors. The greatest strengths were expressed as interpersonal skills (Mean = 2.55, SD = 0.55) and talents/interests (Mean = 2.63, SD = 0.35). However, these scores were quite elevated (signifying limited strengths) and varied only slightly with the other items in the subset.

Table 21: Percent of Adult Needs and Strengths Assessment scores
by level at NGRI admission

Category	Item	0	1	2	3
Problem Presentation					
	Psychosis	0.0	4.1	46.6	49.3
	Impulsivity	38.4	32.9	23.3	5.5
	Depression/ Anxiety	0.0	17.8	65.8	16.4
	Antisocial	16.4	41.1	34.2	8.2
	Substance Abuse	19.2	8.2	24.7	47.9
	Adjustment to Trauma	50.7	31.5	17.8	0.0
	Personality Disorder	27.4	32.9	35.6	4.1
Problem Modifiers					
	Situational Consistency	0.0	0.0	39.7	60.3
	Temporal Consistency	0.0	1.4	87.7	11.0
	Motivation for Treatment	0.0	13.7	76.7	9.6
Risk Behaviors					
	Danger to Self	5.5	26.0	46.6	21.9
	Danger to Other	1.4	9.6	32.9	56.2
	Sexually Inappropriate	75.3	13.7	11.0	0.0
	Social Behavior	1.4	23.3	74.0	1.4
	Crime	0.0	1.4	32.9	65.8
	Victimization	57.5	23.3	13.7	5.5

Table Continues

Table 21: Percent of Adult Needs and Strengths Assessment scores by level at NGRI admission -- Continued

Category	Item	0	1	2	3
Problem Presentation					
	Intellectual Functioning	49.3	42.5	6.8	1.4
	Knowledge of Illness	0.0	9.6	79.5	11.0
	Physical/Medical	38.4	27.4	34.2	0.0
	Family Functioning	11.0	47.9	41.1	0.0
	Employment/ Education	0.0	21.9	74.0	4.1
	Independent Living Skills	15.1	43.8	38.4	2.7
	Residential Stability	11.0	56.2	30.1	2.7
Care Intensity and Organization					
	Resources	1.4	24.7	69.9	4.1
	Organization	0.0	4.1	74.0	21.9
	Monitoring	0.0	5.5	72.6	21.9
	Treatment Intensity	0.0	1.4	75.3	23.3
	Service Permanence	5.5	32.9	57.5	4.1
	Self-Care	9.6	31.5	58.9	0.0
	Medical Complications	0.0	11.0	68.5	20.5

Table Continues

Table 21: Percent of Adult Needs and Strengths Assessment scores by level at NGRI admission -- Continued

Category Item	0	1	2	3
Family/Caregiver Capacities				
Caregiver Health	24.7	32.9	41.1	1.4
Caregiver Involvement	6.8	30.1	61.6	1.4
Caregiver Knowledge	0.0	24.7	72.6	2.7
Caregiver Safety	49.3	39.7	9.6	1.4
Strengths				
Family	0.0	4.1	24.7	71.2
Interpersonal Skills	0.0	2.7	39.7	57.5
Relationship Permanence	0.0	1.4	26.0	72.6
Vocational	0.0	1.4	30.1	68.5
Spirituality/ Religious	0.0	4.1	11.0	84.9
Talents/Interests	0.0	2.7	31.5	65.8
Inclusion Community	0.0	0.0	13.7	86.3

The item scores are further delineated in Table 21 that shows the percent of the sample that scored at each of the four severity levels. For example, nearly 50% of the sample scored '2' on the Psychosis item. This result would suggest that half of the sample needed treatment and monitoring for psychotic symptoms and would most likely meet the criteria for a severe mental illness. Comparable breakdowns are present for each of the ANSA items at admission.

ANSA Scores at Discharge

The item scores were considerably lower and more consistent at discharge (see Table 22). Only seven items were elevated beyond the 1-point threshold. The acquittees continued to have potential problems with psychotic symptoms (Mean = 1.04, SD = 0.26), criminal behavior (Mean = 1.00, SD = 0.00), educational and vocational functioning (Mean = 1.29, SD = 0.57), and limited resources (Mean = 1.52, SD = 0.60). They also tended to have elevated transportation needs (Mean = 1.12, SD = 0.37). Their caregivers continued to have both limited knowledge of their illnesses (Mean = 1.14, SD = 0.71) and moderate involvement in their care (Mean = 1.05, SD = 0.72). The acquittees' gains tended to be consistent across situations (Mean = 1.98, SD = 0.71) and over time (Mean = 1.90, 0.67).

Table 23 shows the distribution of ANSA item scores at discharge. Each column contains the percent of the sample that met a particular severity level for each item. For example, almost 90% of the sample obtained a '0' on the Sexually Inappropriate Behavior item on the ANSA. This result suggests that few acquittees acted out sexually during the period of time preceding their discharge or episodes of sexual misconduct were not documented in the records.

Table 22: Adult Needs and Strengths Assessment scores
at NGRI discharge

Category	Item	Minimum	Maximum	Mean	S.D.
Problem Presentation					
	Psychosis	0	2	1.04	0.26
	Impulsivity	0	1	0.33	0.47
	Depression/ Anxiety	0	2	0.85	0.52
	Antisocial	0	2	0.52	0.53
	Substance Abuse	0	1	0.12	0.33
	Adjustment to Trauma	0	1	0.18	0.39
	Personality Disorder	0	2	0.53	0.63
Problem Modifiers					
	Situational Consistency	1	3	1.98	0.71
	Temporal Consistency	1	3	1.90	0.67
	Motivation for Treatment	0	2	0.79	0.44
Risk Behaviors					
	Danger to Self	0	1	0.53	0.50
	Danger to Other	0	1	0.74	0.44
	Sexually Inappropriate	0	1	0.12	0.33
	Social Behavior	0	2	0.63	0.54
	Crime	1	1	1.00	0.00
	Victimization	0	1	0.25	0.43

Table Continues

Table 22: Adult Needs and Strengths Assessment scores
at NGRI discharge -- Continued

Category	Item	Minimum	Maximum	Mean	S.D.
Problem Presentation					
	Intellectual Functioning	0	3	0.55	0.71
	Knowledge of Illness	0	2	0.9	0.56
	Physical/Medical	0	2	0.42	0.64
	Family Functioning	0	2	0.96	0.72
	Employment/ Education	0	3	1.29	0.57
	Independent Living Skills	0	2	0.48	0.58
	Residential Stability	0	2	0.79	0.50
Care Intensity and Organization					
	Resources	0	2	1.52	0.60
	Organization	0	2	0.70	0.64
	Monitoring	0	2	0.89	0.46
	Treatment Intensity	0	2	1.12	0.37
	Service Permanence	0	2	0.73	0.51
	Self-Care	0	2	0.34	0.53
	Medical Complications	0	2	0.85	0.52

Table Continues

Table 22: Adult Needs and Strengths Assessment scores
at NGRI discharge -- Continued

Category Item	Minimum	Maximum	Mean	S.D.
Family/Caregiver Capacities				
Caregiver Health	0	2	0.73	0.75
Caregiver Involvement	0	2	1.05	0.72
Caregiver Knowledge	0	2	1.14	0.71
Caregiver Safety	0	1	0.14	0.35
Strengths				
Family	1	3	2.44	0.76
Interpersonal Skills	1	3	2.16	0.62
Relationship Permanence	1	3	2.53	0.60
Vocational	1	3	2.52	0.56
Spirituality/ Religious	1	3	2.82	0.45
Talents/Interests	1	3	2.36	0.65
Inclusion in the Community	1	3	2.82	0.42

Table 23: Percent of Adult Needs and Strengths Assessment scores by level at NGRI discharge

Category Item	0	1	2	3
Problem Presentation				
Psychosis	1.4	93.2	5.5	0.0
Impulsivity	67.1	32.9	0.0	0.0
Depression/ Anxiety	21.9	71.2	6.8	0.0
Antisocial	49.3	49.3	1.4	0.0
Substance Abuse	87.7	12.3	0.0	0.0
Adjustment to Trauma	82.2	17.8	0.0	0.0
Personality Disorder	53.4	39.7	6.8	0.0
Problem Modifiers				
Situational Consistency	26.0	50.7	23.3	0.0
Temporal Consistency	0.0	27.4	54.8	17.8
Motivation for Treatment	21.9	76.7	1.4	0.0
Risk Behaviors				
Danger to Self	46.6	53.4	0.0	0.0
Danger to Others	26.0	74.0	0.0	0.0
Sexually Inappropriate	87.7	12.3	0.0	0.0
Social Behavior	39.7	57.5	2.7	0.0
Crime	0.0	100.0	0.0	0.0
Victimization	75.3	24.7	0.0	0.0

Table Continues

Table 23: Percent of Adult Needs and Strengths Assessment scores by level at NGRI discharge -- Continued

Category Item	0	1	2	3
Problem Presentation				
Intellectual Functioning	56.2	34.2	8.2	1.4
Knowledge of Illness	19.2	68.5	12.3	0.0
Physical/Medical	65.8	26.0	8.2	0.0
Family Functioning	27.4	49.3	23.3	0.0
Employment/ Education	4.1	64.4	30.1	1.4
Independent Living Skills	56.2	39.7	4.1	0.0
Residential Stability	24.7	71.2	4.1	0.0
Care Intensity and Organization				
Resources	5.5	37.0	57.5	0.0
Organization	39.7	50.7	9.6	0.0
Monitoring	16.4	78.1	5.5	0.0
Treatment Intensity	1.4	84.9	13.7	0.0
Service Permanence	30.1	67.1	2.7	0.0
Self-Care	68.5	28.8	2.7	0.0
Medical Complications	21.9	71.2	6.8	0.0

Table Continues

Table 23: Percent of Adult Needs and Strengths Assessment scores by level at NGRI discharge -- Continued

Category Item	0	1	2	3
Family/Caregiver Capacities				
Caregiver Health	45.2	37.0	17.8	0.0
Caregiver Involvement	23.3	47.9	28.8	0.0
Caregiver Knowledge	19.2	47.9	32.9	0.0
Caregiver Safety	49.3	39.7	9.6	1.4
Strengths				
Family	0.0	16.4	23.3	60.3
Interpersonal Skills	0.0	12.3	58.9	28.8
Relationship Permanence	0.0	5.5	35.6	58.9
Vocational	0.0	2.7	42.5	54.8
Spirituality/ Religious	0.0	2.7	12.3	84.9
Talents/Interests	0.0	9.6	45.2	45.2
Inclusion in the Community	0.0	1.4	15.1	83.6

Clinical Progress from Admission to Discharge

Figures 3 through 9 depict the clinical progress made during the NGRI hospitalization. Statistically significant improvement was made on all ANSA items except Intellectual Functioning, Spirituality, and Inclusion in the Community. The degree of the improvement appeared to depend most upon the extent of the original impairment (see Table 24). Clinical improvement over time predicted neither re-arrest nor re-hospitalization.

Figure 3: Change in ANSA scores from admission
to discharge: problem presentation

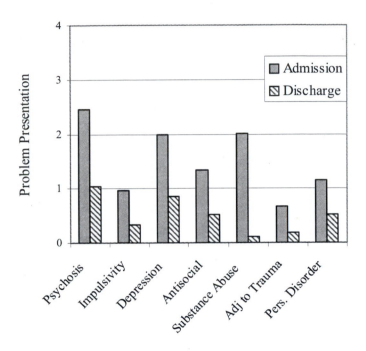

Figure 4: Change in ANSA scores from admission to discharge: problem modifiers

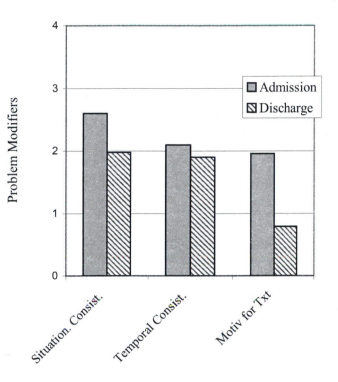

Figure 5: Change in ANSA scores from admission
to discharge: risk behaviors

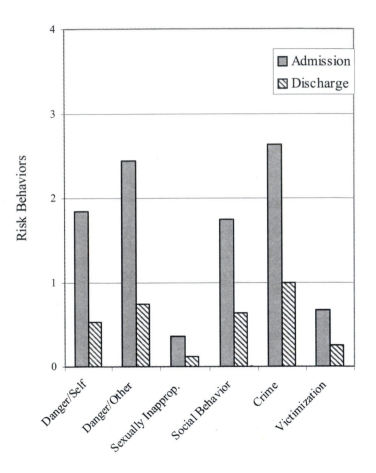

Figure 6: Change in ANSA scores from admission to
discharge: functioning

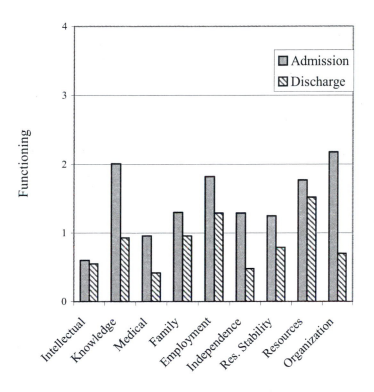

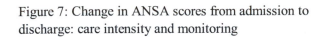

Figure 7: Change in ANSA scores from admission to discharge: care intensity and monitoring

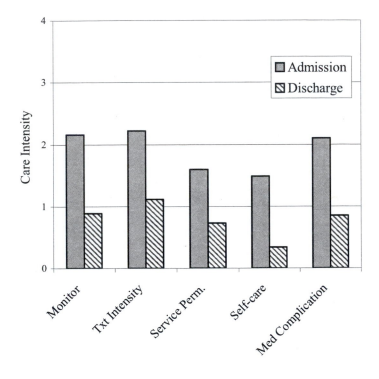

Figure 8: Change in ANSA scores from admission to discharge: caregiver/family capacity

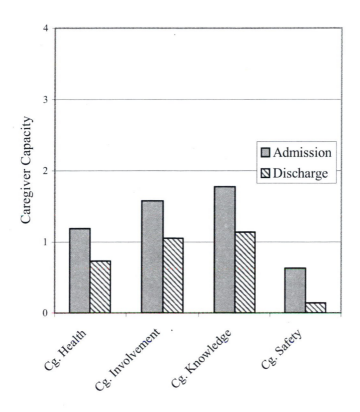

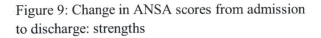

Figure 9: Change in ANSA scores from admission to discharge: strengths

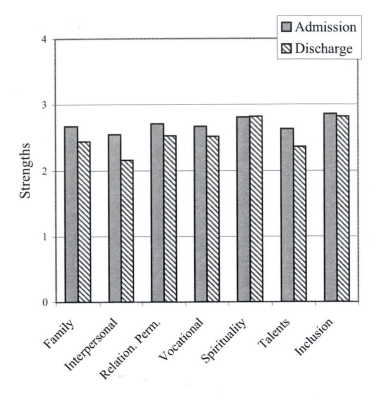

Table 24: Clinical progress of acquittees from admission to discharge

Item	Mean Difference	t-score	df	p-value
Problem Presentation				
Psychosis	-1.41	20.19	72	$p < 0.001$
Impulsivity	-0.63	7.72	72	$p < 0.001$
Depression/ Anxiety	-1.14	14.01	72	$p < 0.001$
Antisocial	-0.82	9.84	72	$p < 0.001$
Substance Abuse	-1.89	14.52	72	$p < 0.001$
Adjustment to Trauma	-0.49	5.64	72	$p < 0.001$
Personality Disorder	-0.63	9.13	72	$p < 0.001$
Problem Modifiers				
Situational Consistency	-0.62	8.20	72	$p < 0.001$
Temporal Consistency	-0.20	2.22	72	$p < 0.05$
Motivation for Treatment	-1.17	14.92	72	$p < 0.001$
Risk Behaviors				
Danger to Self	-1.32	13.80	72	$p < 0.001$
Danger to Other	-1.70	21.32	72	$p < 0.001$
Sexually Inappropriate	-0.24	3.87	72	$p < 0.001$
Social Behavior	-1.12	16.01	72	$p < 0.001$
Crime	-1.64	27.53	72	$p < 0.001$
Victimization	-0.42	5.64	72	$p < 0.001$

Table Continues

Table 24: Clinical progress of acquittees from admission to discharge
Continued

Item	Mean Difference	t-score	df	p-value
Problem Presentation				
Intellectual Functioning	-0.05	1.42	72	p < 0.20
Knowledge of Illness	-1.08	13.17	72	p < 0.001
Physical/ Medical	-0.54	6.83	72	p < 0.001
Family Functioning	-0.34	5.78	72	p < 0.001
Employment/ Education	-0.53	6.83	72	p < 0.001
Independent Living Skills	-0.81	9.86	72	p < 0.001
Residential Stability	-0.46	5.98	72	p < 0.001
Care Intensity and Organization				
Resources	-0.25	4.04	72	p < 0.001
Organization	-1.48	17.82	72	p < 0.001
Monitoring	-1.27	17.94	72	p < 0.001
Treatment Intensity	-1.10	15.48	72	p < 0.001
Service Permanence	-0.87	9.19	72	p < 0.001
Self-Care	-1.15	14.45	72	p < 0.001
Medical Complications	0.29	15.16	72	p < 0.001

Table Continues

Table 24: Clinical progress of acquittees from admission to discharge
Continued

Item	Mean Difference	t-score	df	p-value
<u>Family/Caregiver Capacities</u>				
Caregiver Health	-0.46	4.77	72	p < 0.001
Caregiver Involvement	-0.53	7.10	72	p < 0.001
Caregiver Knowledge	-0.64	7.92	72	p < 0.001
Caregiver Safety	-0.49	6.73	72	p < 0.001
<u>Strengths</u>				
Family	-0.23	4.68	72	p < 0.001
Interpersonal Skills	-0.39	6.34	72	p < 0.001
Relationship Permanence	-0.18	3.63	72	p < 0.01
Vocational	-0.15	2.62	72	p < 0.05
Spirituality/ Religious	0.01	-0.22	72	p < 1.0
Talents/ Interests	-0.27	3.72	72	p < 0.001
Inclusion in the Community	-0.04	1.00	72	p < 0.50

Prediction of Re-Arrest and Re-Hospitalization Using ANSA Items

Re-Arrest

Odds ratios calculated for each ANSA item's correspondence with re-arrest demonstrated fifteen statistically significant comparisons (see Table 25). No discharge ANSA items served as predictors given their limited variability. For every significant item, acquittees who were rated three were compared with acquittees who were rated zero, one, or two; acquittees who were rated three or two were compared with acquittees who were rated zero or one; and acquittees who were rated three, two or one were compared with acquittees who were rated zero. Given that the ANSA contains forty-two distinct items, one hundred and twenty-six comparisons were therefore conducted.

3 vs. 2, 1, or 0: Seven of the fifteen statistically significant results stemmed from comparisons of individuals rated three versus less than three. Persons rated three on Medication Compliance were 10.93 times more likely to be re-arrested than persons rated below three (p < 0.01). Similar but less dramatic results were found for acquittees rated three on Motivation for Treatment (8.50, p < 0.01), Caregiver Involvement (6.90, p < 0.01), Crime (6.90, p < 0.01), or Substance Abuse (4.95, p < 0.01). All acquittees rated three on Service Permanence were re-arrested (p < 0.01) thereby producing an infinite odds ratio. Similarly, no acquittees rated zero, one or two on Spirituality/Religiosity were re-arrested (p < 0.05) thereby providing an undefined odds ratio.

<u>3 or 2 vs. 1 or 0</u>: In terms of comparisons between acquittees rated three or two versus zero or one, four statistically significant results were obtained. No acquittees rated zero or one on Substance Abuse ($p < 0.01$) or Motivation for Treatment ($p < 0.05$) were re-arrested, thereby producing undefined odds ratios. Individuals rated three or two on Antisocial Behavior (4.94, $p < 0.01$) or Service Permanence (5.06, $p < 0.05$) were significantly more likely to be re-arrested than their comparison group.

<u>3, 2, or 1 vs. 0</u>: Finally, three comparisons between persons rated three, two or one on an item versus individuals rate zero produced significant results. Acquittees rated higher on Danger to Self (0.11, $p < 0.05$) and Caregiver Health (0.35, $p < 0.05$) were less likely to be re-arrested. Given that no acquittees rated zero on Substance Abuse were re-arrested, the odds ratio was undefined ($p < 0.05$).

Table 25: Prediction of re-arrest using ANSA items at admission

Item	Percent Re-arrested (N = 73)				Odds Ratios		
	0	1	2	3	0 vs 123	01 vs. 23	012 vs.3
Substance Abuse	0	0	28	43	∞*	∞**	4.95**
Antisocial	0	20	48	33	--	4.94**	1.3
Service Permanence	0	13	33	100	--	5.06*	∞**
Motivation for Treatment	--	0	27	71	--	∞*	8.50**
Impulsivity	21	21	41	50	1.66	2.80	2.83
Medical Complications	--	0	24	53	--	--	4.38*
Knowledge	--	0	24	75	--	--	10.93**
Victimization	17	41	40	50	3.61	2.41	2.83
Caregiver Health	44	25	20	0	0.35*	0.48	--
Social Behavior	0	18	30	100	--	2.24	--
Caregiver Knowledge	--	17	30	50	--	2.24	2.74
Personality Disorder	10	33	38	0	4.63	1.79	--
Organization	--	0	26	38	--	--	1.84
Family	--	0	22	31	--	--	1.89
Spirituality	--	0	0	32	--	--	∞*
Resources	0	39	24	33	--	0.54	1.34
Adjustment to Trauma	22	43	15	--	1.81	0.42	--
Psychosis	--	0	24	33	--	--	1.81
Monitoring	--	50	25	31	--	0.35	1.27
Depression/Anxiety	--	38	27	17	--	0.53	0.48
Danger to Self	75	26	26	19	0.11*	0.59	0.54
Living Skills	0	31	36	0	--	1.65	--
Talents/Interests	--	0	9	38	--	--	6.90**

* p < 0.05
**p < 0.01

Table Continues

108

Table 25: Prediction of re-arrest using ANSA items at admission
Continued

Item	Percent Re-arrested (N = 73)				Odds Ratios		
	0	1	2	3	0 vs 123	01 vs. 23	012 vs.3
Caregiver Involvement	20	23	31	0	1.55	1.53	--
Interpersonal	--	50	24	29	--	0.37	1.15
Caregiver Safety	19	34	43	0	2.24	1.69	--
Sexually Inappropriate	24	40	38	--	2.06	1.69	--
Crime	--	0	8	38	--	--	6.90**
Treatment Consistency	--	0	30	13	--	--	0.35
Treatment Intensity	--	0	22	47	--	--	3.26
Relationship Permanence	--	0	32	26	--	--	0.84
Vocational/ Educational	--	0	18	32	--	--	2.24
Self Care	0	39	26	--	--	0.80	--
Family	13	29	30	--	2.89	1.25	--
Intensity of Services	31	23	40	0	0.73	1.36	--
Employment	--	25	26	67	--	1.17	5.78
Residential Stability	13	29	32	0	2.89	1.14	--
Danger to Others	0	29	33	24	--	1.15	0.71
Physical/Medical	21	35	28	--	1.66	1.05	--
Situational Consistency	--	--	21	32	--	--	1.79
Well-Being	--	--	33	27	--	--	0.75
Inclusion	--	--	20	29	--	--	1.60

**p < 0.01

109

Re-Hospitalization

3 vs. 2, 1, or 0:   Table 26 summarizes the odds ratios calculated for each ANSA item's capacity to predict re-hospitalization. There were seven statistically significant comparisons ($p < 0.05$). Five of these results were found for comparisons between acquittees rated three versus those individuals rated less than three. Acquittees rated three on Resources were 13.57 times more likely to be re-hospitalized than persons ranked less than three. For the Caregiver Health, Caregiver Involvement, and Caregiver Safety items, the group rated three was infinitely more likely to be re-hospitalized than the comparison group. In other words, one hundred percent of the group rated three was re-hospitalized.   Those acquittees rated three on Psychosis were 3.24 times more likely than the others to be re-hospitalized.

3 or 2 vs. 1 or 0: The final statistically significant results stemmed from comparisons of groups rated two or three versus groups rated zero or one. Acquittees rated two or three on Employment and Educational Functioning produced an undefined odds ratio when compared with the others. This result stemmed from the lack of acquittees within the group rated zero or one being re-hospitalized. Lastly, acquittees rated two or three on the antisocial item were 0.25 times less likely to be re-hospitalized than the others.

Table 26: Prediction of re-hospitalization using ANSA items at admission

Item	Percent Re-arrested (N = 73)				Odds Ratios		
	0	1	2	3	0 vs 123	01 vs. 23	012 vs.3
Resources	0	11	14	67	--	1.70	13.56*
Caregiver Health	17	8	17	100	0.85	1.78	∞*
Caregiver Inv.	0	14	16	100	--	1.68	∞*
Caregiver Safety	11	21	0	100	1.87	0.79	∞*
Psychosis	--	0	9	22	--	--	3.24*
Family	--	0	6	19	--	--	4.76
Inclusion in Community	--	--	30	13	--	--	0.34
Caregiver Knowledge	--	11	15	50	--	1.57	6.10
Residential Stability	13	17	9	50	1.27	0.73	6.10
Treatment Consistency	--	0	17	0	--	--	--
Knowledge	--	14	17	0	--	1.07	--
Monitoring	--	0	13	25	--	--	2.38
Substance Abuse	14	17	6	20	1.08	1.01	2.13
Danger to Self	0	16	21	6	--	1.27	0.31
Interpersonal	--	0	10	19	--	--	2.20
Motivation for Treatment	--	20	13	29	--	0.67	2.53
Vocational/Educ.	--	0	9	18	--	--	2.30
Employment	--	0	19	33	--	∞*	3.00
Service Permanence	25	17	12	33	0.51	0.71	3.00
Personality Dis.	15	8	23	0	1.01	2.03	--
Well-being	--	--	0	16	--	--	--
Living Skills	9	13	21	0	1.92	1.90	--
Medical Complications	--	13	14	20	--	1.27	1.56

* p < 0.05   Table Continues

111

Table 26: Prediction of re-hospitalization using ANSA items at admission

Item	Percent Re-arrested (N = 73)				Odds Ratios		
	0	1	2	3	0 vs 123	01 vs. 23	012 vs.3
Victimization	17	18	0	25	0.74	0.38	1.97
Impulsivity	18	8	18	25	0.71	1.51	1.97
Danger to Others	0	14	13	17	--	1.27	1.44
Crime	--	0	13	17	--	--	1.47
Organization	--	0	15	19	--	--	1.41
Social Behavior	0	24	13	0	--	0.51	--
Service Intensity	14	16	20	0	1.20	1.14	--
Treatment Intensity	--	0	15	18	--	--	1.29
Spirituality Religion	--	0	25	15	--	--	0.76
Situational Consistency	--	--	14	16	--	--	1.18
Depression/Anx.	--	15	15	17	--	0.97	1.16
Talents/Interests	--	0	17	15	--	--	0.90
Antisocial	17	23	4	17	0.87	0.25*	1.14
Relational Permanence	--	0	16	15	--	--	1.01
Family	13	11	20	--	1.27	1.90	--
Physical/Medical	18	15	12	--	0.71	0.68	--
Self Care	14	13	16	--	1.07	1.26	--
Sexually. Inappropriate	16	10	13	--	0.64	0.79	--
Adjustment to Trauma	14	17	15	--	1.28	1.03	--

* $p < 0.05$

Logistic Regression Model Using ANSA Items to Predict Re-Arrest and Re-Hospitalization
Re-Arrest

Table 27 outlines the four items entered into the logistic regression model predicting re-arrest: Substance Abuse (Wald = 9.82, p < 0.01), Crime (Wald = 9.71, p < 0.01), Antisocial Behavior (Wald = 4.28, p < 0.05), and Motivation for Care (Wald = 3.40, p < 0.10). These variables accounted for 84.9% of the variability (see Table 28). The model had more false negatives than false positives (69.6% versus 92.0% correct prediction, respectively).

Table 27: Logistic regression model using ANSA items to predict re-arrest

Step Item	Wald	α	Cox & Snell R^2	Nagelkerke R^2
1 Substance Abuse	9.82	0.00	0.24	0.33
2 Crime	9.71	0.00	0.38	0.53
3 Antisocial Behavior	4.28	0.04	0.42	0.59
4 Motivation for Care	3.40	0.07	0.46	0.64

Table 28: Accuracy of model predicting re-arrest

| | | Predicted | | |
		No	Yes	Percentage Correct
	No	46	4	92.0
Actual	Yes	7	16	69.6
	Total	--	--	84.9

Re-Hospitalization

Only one item, Employment (Wald = 3.70, $p < 0.05$), was entered into the logistic regression model predicting re-hospitalization (see Table 29). Nonetheless, the model correctly predicted 83.6% of the cases (see Table 30). There were considerably more false negatives than false positives (9.1% versus 96.8% correct prediction, respectively).

Table 29: Logistic regression model using ANSA items to predict re-hospitalization

Step	Item	Wald	Significance	Cox & Snell R^2	Nagelkerke R^2
1	Employment	3.70	0.05	0.061	0.12

Table 30: Accuracy of model predicting re-hospitalization

		Predicted		
		No	Yes	Percentage Correct
	No	60	2	96.8
Actual	Yes	10	1	9.1
	Total	--	--	83.6

Veteran vs. Non-Veteran Comparison

Table 31 depicts the factors that produced statistically significant results when compared across groups. At admission, veteran NGRI acquittees (N = 10) differed significantly from non-veterans (N = 63) on a variety of items. Veterans tended to abuse substances more severely (t = -3.04, p < 0.01), have greater difficulty caring for themselves (t = -2.23, p < 0.05), and live in more threatening environments (t = -2.27, p < 0.03) than persons who had not served in the military. At discharge, they demonstrated more severe psychotic symptoms (t = -2.13, p < 0.05), greater variation in their symptoms over time (t = 2.62, p < 0.01), and less likelihood to be victimized (t = 4.98, p < 0.01). They tended to have greater difficulties acquiring and sustaining employment (t = -2.58, p < 0.05), organizing themselves and their lives (t = 2.37, p < 0.05), taking their medications (t = -2.38, p < 0.05), and attending to their overall well-being (t = -2.31, p < 0.05). In addition, they were more isolated from the broader community (t = 3.68, p < 0.01) and tended to be older (t = -3.08, p < 0.01).

Table 31: Veteran and non-veteran NGRI acquittee comparison on actuarial variables, ANSA items, and recidivism

Type	Item	Veteran Mean	SD	T-score
Demographic Characteristics at Admission				
	Age	51.50	15.11	-3.08**
ANSA Items at Admission				
	Substance Abuse	2.60	0.52	-3.04**
	Self Care	1.80	0.42	-2.23*
	Safety of Caregiving Environment	0.90	0.32	-2.27*
ANSA Items at Discharge Discharge				
	Psychotic Symptoms	1.20	0.42	-2.13*
	Temporal Consistency	2.40	0.52	-2.62*
	Victimization	0.00	0.00	4.98**
	Employment Functioning	1.70	0.68	-2.58*
	Organization	1.10	0.57	-2.37*
	Medication Compliance	1.20	0.42	-2.74*
	Well-Being	3.00	0.00	-2.31*
	Inclusion in Community	3.00	0.00	-3.68**

*p < 0.05
**p < 0.01

116

CHAPTER 5

Policy and Research Implications

The acquittees in the present study were similar to past samples in terms of their clinical characteristics and service utilization histories. They demonstrated significant clinical improvement across almost all domains during the NGRI hospital stay and recidivated equal to or less than most prior samples. A variety of individual and community strengths and vulnerabilities were identified as predictors of re-arrest and re-hospitalization. These factors were incorporated into models that accounted for nearly 85% of the variability in the dependent variables. These results suggest that the present system of treatment and conditional release in Illinois, though underdeveloped in many capacities, appears to have improved upon practices used in some other states.

NGRI acquittees occupy a unique position within the criminal justice and mental health systems, both for the intensity of the responses they elicit and the complexity of factors influencing their release into the community. Although insanity defense pleas and especially insanity acquittals are rare phenomena, NGRI acquittees embody a series of ambiguities that profoundly impact administrators, health services researchers, and clinicians. Their existence challenges criminal justice and mental health professionals to integrate large, often bureaucratic systems, more clearly define their respective roles in working with shared clients, and most importantly, balance the need to provide services in less restrictive settings while protecting the community and the acquittees themselves from undue harm. The present study is an attempt to address this last challenge. By tracking the criminal and hospital recidivism patterns of seventy-three NGRI acquittees for up to eighteen years, conducting detailed retrospective chart reviews, and administering a comprehensive outcomes assessment and clinical decision making tool, the present study assesses the following factors: the acquittees' clinical characteristics; their clinical progress during the index hospitalization; the variables that predict re-arrest and re-hospitalization, including the integration of such factors into predictive models; the commonalities and differences between veteran and non-veteran NGRI acquittees; and lastly, the challenges that will most likely shape researchers studying similar issues in the future.

Individual Characteristics
The acquittees in the present study resembled typical NGRI samples. They tended to be male, poorly educated, and somewhat socially isolated. Most of the subjects had never married nor served in the military, and were unemployed at the time of the index crime. Similar to prior results, the majority of acquittees had been arrested and hospitalized previously. Although prior samples averaged between thirty and thirty-six years of age, the present sample tended to be roughly 40 years old.[132]

More than eighty percent of the index crime charges were for violent offenses. Given the controversy surrounding the insanity defense, difficulties using it successfully, and the restrictions central to most NGRI dispositions, one would expect that the defense would usually be used in cases involving serious crimes.[133] Individuals, who commit mild offenses and may meet the criteria for insanity, may be advised to plea bargain or plead guilty instead of using the somewhat unpredictable defense.

The majority of acquittees in the preset study were diagnosed with a psychotic disorder at the time of the NGRI admission. However, the most common diagnoses were substance use disorders. More than seventy percent of acquittees had comorbid substance use and other psychiatric disorders. Past studies typically demonstrated comparable rates of psychotic symptoms but less chemical abuse. It is unclear what factors account for the high levels of substance use among this sample. Regardless, the programmatic implications are clear. Conditional release programs need comprehensive dual-diagnosis treatments in order to be effective.[134]

The lack of persons diagnosed with an anxiety disorder in the present study is noteworthy. Only one individual was diagnosed at admission with one of the many anxiety disorders. This result differs considerably from previous studies. The frequency of both mood and personality disorders resembles prior results, approximating 40% for each group.

Clinical Progress from NGRI Admission to Discharge
Fairly consistent patterns of individual and community strengths and vulnerabilities emerged at admission. The acquittees tended to experience frequent and severe psychotic symptoms and intensive affective disturbance, and rely upon psychoactive substances presumably in order to self-medicate. They were typically dangerous both to self and others, and demonstrated strong criminal tendencies. Their difficulties tended to be consistent across situations and over time.

They appeared to know little about their illnesses, resist taking prescribed medications, have limited socio-economic resources, and need frequent and intensive monitoring. Their caregivers tended to know little about their illnesses and have only limited involvement in their treatment. At admission, strengths that would later emerge appeared dormant, inhibited, or perhaps simply unrecognized.

During the NGRI inpatient stay, the acquittees demonstrated marked clinical progress. They showed statistically significant improvement across all items except three. Their scores for the Intellectual Functioning, Spirituality, and Inclusion in the Community items were relatively stable from admission to discharge. Improved medication compliance and participation in treatment appeared to have significant effects on the acquittees' psychotic symptoms. They seemed to have learned about their illnesses and improved their self-care. They became less dangerous toward themselves and others, demanded less intensive monitoring, and demonstrated particular strengths relating to people and developing hobbies. Although the acquittees revealed marked reductions in substance use, criminal activity, and dangerousness to self and others, it is difficult to assess the extent to which this progress results simply from being in a more restrictive setting or is attributable to gains made through treatment. One way to assess this distinction is to examine the post-discharge recidivism patterns. If the improvements are merely setting effects, then high rates of post-conditional release criminal activity would be observed.

Criminal Recidivism
Correlates. Compared to previous samples, the acquittees in the present study recidivated within the low average range, accounting for the extended follow-up period. Nearly one third of the sample was re-arrested after being released into the community and half of those arrested committed violent crimes. Less than one quarter of the total number of re-arrests (average between three and four per recidivate) were for violent offenses however. Anecdotally, Office of Mental Health staff reported that these incidents rarely lead to injury and extremely rarely involve strangers. They claim that these arrests, commonly labeled as domestic abuse and therefore registered as violent crimes, typically involve domestic disturbances that involve property damage and shouting, but little violence. Given that rap sheets were not reviewed during the present study, however, such observations could not be cross-validated. It is noteworthy, however, that nearly 65% of violent re-arrests were domestically related.

Similar factors found in previous studies were associated with re-arrest. For example, substance use, antisocial tendencies, medication non-compliance, and prior criminal behavior were related to increased criminal recidivism. A series of additional factors also were observed. Persons, who experienced frequent disruptions in their treatment relationships, were more likely to be re-arrested. Given trends within the broader mental health system toward community based care and the subsequent fragmentation that can occasionally occur, improving linkages between service providers and reducing staff turn-over should be primary systemic objectives.[135] Patients who move from one agency to another or must tolerate transient clinical relationships appear to be at significant risk to commit criminal offenses.

Individuals who demonstrate little motivation to solicit and participate in clinical services also were likely to recidivate. Clinical engagement is a central component in protecting acquittees and members of their communities. Conflicting opinions arise however when one tries to improve motivation for treatment. Mandated conditional release programs can be envisioned both as assurance that engagement will occur and coercive measures that actually serve to reduce individuals' motivation for treatment by stifling their autonomy.[136]   Given the security concerns surrounding this population and the generally accepted success of conditional release programs in reducing recidivism, it is unlikely that discharge mandates would be lessened. Therefore, clinicians need to develop effective ways to work within the parameters of treatment contracts in order to promote patient agency and sustain therapeutic relationships.[137]

Self-harming tendencies were inversely related to re-arrest. This result may be a measure of internalizing versus externalizing tendencies. Persons who self-harm may be less likely to act out their distress and therefore fail to provoke the attention of the police. The present study did not assess self-harming behavior after conditional release. Therefore, it is possible that these individuals are actually more threatening to themselves than members of their communities. They may display aggressive patterns of acting out; however, they may serve both as the subjects and objects of their aggression.

In addition, the psychological and physical health of the acquittees' caregivers appears to relate to re-arrest. Caregivers may play a central role in providing stability and support to vulnerable individuals.[138] The instability created by ill caregivers can be understood in relation to the previous discussion surrounding service impermanence. NGRI acquittees appear to demand high levels of environmental stability. In-house care and respite services may be effective ways to support caregivers and therefore prevent psychologically and financially costly recidivism.

Two additional factors were inversely related to re-arrest. Acquittees who were affiliated with a religious community or had clearly defined talents and interests were less likely to recidivate. These activities appear to serve a protective function.[139] Investing in projects and persons outside of oneself and engaging with the outside world seem to promote pro-social behavior. A variety of studies suggest that strengths-based service planning produces better results.[140] Therefore, during inpatient stays, a central role of treatment planning should be identifying and nurturing patient strengths. In addition, discharge planning should not only include linking patients with community mental health centers but also arts facilities, athletic teams and social clubs when appropriate.

In summary, the following programmatic changes may reduce criminal recidivism by addressing the factors most closely linked with re-arrest. Each intervention corresponds to a previously identified correlate.

- Comprehensive treatment programs addressing comorbid substance use and mental disorder.

- Improved linkages between community providers and staff retention in order to create more stable and consistent treatment relationships.

- Development of more sophisticated and reliable means for engaging acquittees and promoting patient autonomy within the context of mandated treatment programs.

- Unique treatment pathways and techniques for monitoring persons with internalizing tendencies.

- Improved supportive services for caregivers.

- Identification and nurturance of patient strengths.

Prediction Model. These individual correlates need not be addressed in isolation. They can be integrated into a model that predicts re-arrest. Successful models use limited numbers of predictors to account for much of the movement in the dependent variable. If one were to include all of the correlates within a given model, one would be wasting resources by duplicating predictive capacities. Therefore, a forward entry conditional approach was used to construct a logistic regression model that would only include those variables that added significantly to the predictive power of the variable or combination of variables previously entered into the model. Four variables, substance abuse, prior criminal behavior, antisocial behavior, and motivation for treatment, were accepted into the model step by step.

It is noteworthy that both prior criminal activity and antisocial behavior were included. Despite the obvious overlap between these two variables, they accounted for a significantly larger aspect of the variance together than either factor did in isolation. Antisocial behavior may address personality components (e.g. interpersonal explosiveness and impulsivity) separate from criminal behavior that nonetheless predict future criminality.

Given that the present model uses only four variables, it is a fairly efficient use of resources. Despite its simplicity, it correctly predicts re-arrest for roughly 85% of the cases. Of particular interest in criminal recidivism studies is the percentage of false negatives that result from a model. In other words, how many people would be re-arrested despite predicting that they would remain crime-free? Using the present four variables, almost ten percent of the cases would be false negatives. If we assume that 52.2% of persons re-arrested would be re-arrested for a violent crime, then we can assume that roughly 5% of the acquittees would be labeled safe and yet commit a violent crime. The extent of the danger demands further study. Given the preponderance of domestic abuse charges and the claim by some OMH staff that these incidents rarely involve actual violence, it is unclear how serious the risk of using such a model would be.

Hospital Recidivism
Accounting for the lengthy follow-up period, the NGRI acquittees in the present study tended to be re-hospitalized equal to or less than acquittees in previous studies. Roughly fifteen percent of the acquittees were re-hospitalized during the study period. Within this group, both the mean and modal number of hospitalizations was one. Similar to prior results, acquittees with more severe psychotic symptoms were more likely to recidivate. Given the cyclical nature of many psychotic disorders and the periodic need for the containment and acute treatment that inpatient units can provide, this result is to be expected.

A series of findings were somewhat unique to the present study however. Those acquittees who had fewer financial resources were more likely to be re-hospitalized. Relative wealth appeared to buffer acquittees from some of the stress factors that may precipitate the onset of more severe clinical episodes. Acquittees living in unsafe environments also recidivated more commonly. Linking acquittees with safe, affordable housing may be an alternative way to preserve the individual's community placement.[141]

Occupational instability was also associated with re-hospitalization. Successful employment obviously relates to the accumulation of financial resources. However, it also typically involves interpersonal interaction and investment in a mission outside of one's immediate concerns, and therefore may serve an organizing role in the acquittees' lives. By incorporating occupational skills development into treatment planning and linking acquittees with workplaces during discharge planning, vulnerable individuals may have additional interpersonal, financial, and personal resources that may help them manage the strains of life in the community.[142]

Numerous caregiver factors were also associated with hospital recidivism. Those acquittees, whose caregivers were psychologically or physically ill and/or uninvolved in the acquittees' treatment, were more likely to be re-hospitalized. Caregivers appear to play a vital role in stabilizing the acquittees' living environments, providing interpersonal contact and promoting therapeutic engagement. If caregivers are ill or uninvolved, the treatment seems to suffer. Respite and other supportive services may help caregivers tolerate the potentially overwhelming experience of managing complicated lives.[143] In addition, involving caregivers in treatment planning and ongoing monitoring may lead to more durable and effective community treatments.

Antisocial behavior was the only variable inversely related to re-hospitalization. Antisocial persons tend not to solicit services and therefore will typically avoid inpatient stays when possible. Engaging these patients in treatment of any kind can be challenging. It would be worthwhile to track their participation in outpatient treatment programs in order to identify which, if any, treatment modalities prove sufficiently engaging.

In summary, the following programmatic changes may reduce hospital recidivism by addressing the factors most closely linked with re-hospitalization. Each intervention corresponds to previously identified correlates.

- Access to safe, affordable housing may reduce stressors that precipitate clinical declines.

- Occupational skills development and connection with workplaces may promote economic stability, interpersonal interaction, and a sense of mission that anchors community living.

- Respite and other supportive services directed toward caregivers, along with involving caregivers in treatment planning and management, may help acquittees tolerate the instability that often accompanies life in the community.

Prediction Model. A forward entry logistic regression model was also created using re-hospitalization as the dependent variable. Only one variable however was accepted into the model. Occupational instability accounted for enough variability in the dependent variable that additional factors could not significantly add to the model's predictive power. Each of the clinical, economic, caregiver, and personality variables were accounted for by simply examining the acquittees' occupational functioning. Even measuring the frequency and severity of the acquittees' psychotic symptoms did not add significantly to the model.

Using this simple approach, almost 85% of the acquittees followed the predicted path. Less than 14% of acquittees expected not to remain in outpatient treatment entered the hospital, and only 1% of acquittees expected to be admitted, remained in the community. The distinction between false negatives and false positives is less pressing when considering hospital versus criminal recidivism since the consequences of incorrect predictions are typically less severe.

Clinical Progress from Admission to Discharge
Given the often exaggerated fears that surround NGRI acquittees and the intensity of public pressure to use conservative standards in monitoring them, one would expect that acquittees would need to be quite healthy to be conditionally released. Consistent with this expectation, clinicians reported greatly reduced symptoms at discharge. Inpatient treatments appear to have substantial impact on the clinical functioning of the acquittees. In fact, the ANSA scores at discharge were so consistently low that no variables correlated with either criminal or hospital recidivism. There simply was not enough variability.

It is conceivable that the clinical progress was attributable to factors other than the efficacy of the treatment. For example, the improvement may result from a setting effect. Such a hypothesis would suggest that the acquittees would become symptomatic upon returning to less restrictive community settings. Given that roughly two-thirds of the patients were neither re-arrested nor re-hospitalized, it seems unlikely that the restrictive placement was the primary agent of change.

A second potential explanation for the improvement concerns the strictures placed on conditional release evaluations. The acquittees in the present study were typically denied conditional release multiple times before being discharged. If conservative discharge thresholds are being utilized, it is possible that clinicians are motivated to minimize their patients' disturbances and highlight their clinical gains. The present study does not provide sufficient data to assess this explanation.

Clinical progress did not appear to protect individuals from re-arrest or re-hospitalization. Those individuals who demonstrated marked improvement were just as likely to recidivate as those who displayed only moderate improvement. Therefore, the prevention of re-arrest and re-hospitalization may depend less upon quality inpatient care than improved service linkages, comprehensive community supports, and consistent monitoring of risk factors.

Relationship between Criminal and Hospital Recidivism
Hypotheses concerning the role of hospitalization in preventing re-arrest demand empirical examination. Such hypotheses are difficult to study however. Ideally, one would match acquittees according to their likelihood to commit a crime after discharge, and then randomly assign them to the hospitalization and control groups. For the control group to be truly a control, however, access to

inpatient units would have to be withheld. Such an intervention is obviously unethical and unsafe.

Therefore, researchers are left to conduct various observational studies that hopefully approximate experimental conditions. Given the inability in the present study to conduct sophisticated analyses of time as a factor, a simple correlation of re-hospitalization and re-arrest was calculated. The two variables were not inversely related as would be hypothesized. In other words, individuals who tended to be admitted into the hospital were equally likely to be re-arrested compared with those individuals who avoided post-release hospital stays.

Comparison of Veteran and Non-Veteran Acquittees
Any conclusions concerning the veteran/non-veteran comparison should be considered largely provisional. There were too few veteran acquittees to obtain generalizable results. Therefore, the following comments suggest additional study.

No significant differences in recidivism patterns were found between veteran and non-veteran groups. It appears that veterans do not have unique treatment and monitoring needs. Rather, the interventions that were described in the previous sections would be particularly suited to these acquittees as suggested by those clinical and community variables that produced significant differences. The veteran acquittees tended to be older, live in more dangerous environments, and use more substances that non-veterans. They had greater difficulty caring for themselves, were poorly organized, and often lived isolated lives. In addition, they tended to experience more frequent and severe psychotic symptoms at discharge. It is unclear the extent to which gender differences account for these findings, given that all of the veteran acquittees were male. However, the most likely hypothesis is that differences between veterans and non-veterans would be even smaller if the researcher had a sufficient sample size to control for gender.

Limitations

Results from the present study should be interpreted with the following limitations in mind. The sample consisted of seventy-three NGRI acquittees released within Cook County, Illinois, between 1 January, 1983, and 31 December, 1995. Although the sample size is larger than samples used in many NGRI studies, it is nonetheless small given the complexity of the analyses conducted. The comparison of veteran (N = 10) and non-veteran acquittees (N = 63) was particularly strained by small cell counts. It would be helpful to collect state-wide data in order to enlarge the sample. Using county level data is problematic not only because of the reduced power of the analyses but also given complications tracking acquittees over time. Although the Department of Health and Human Services' database provided statewide hospitalization logs, the Public Defender's database was limited to Cook County. Therefore, if an acquittee were arrested outside of Cook County and the incident was not documented in the clinical chart, the arrest was missed. It is reasonable to expect that the observed recidivism rates in this study and others are somewhat deflated given difficulties integrating data across regions.

Furthermore, regional public databases are notoriously poor and when possible should be evaluated against searches within the National Crime Information Computer.[144] Mistakes and omissions often result from multiple persons entering the data, staffing resources being directed toward more pressing concerns, excessive amounts of paper work, and shifting political contexts that make long-term research initiatives difficult to sustain. In the present study, twenty acquittee charts were not located. Seven of these charts had been shipped to other facilities following a transfer of care. Difficulties finding the rest of the charts most likely stemmed from staff reductions within the central state forensic, mental health facility and the relocation of the medical records room due to budgetary constraints.

The inability to account for time at risk was the most salient limitation of the public databases. Without reviewing rap sheets and other records that would have required written consents, the researcher could not determine when acquittees were being held in jail or prison following an arrest. For some individuals, the necessary dates were clearly documented; however, for many others, the data were sparse and sometimes contradictory. Therefore, it was impossible to account for time at risk reliably.

Furthermore, given the complexity of these cases and the difficulties accessing reliable data, many potentially confounding variables exist. Most notably, the study did not account for variability in the treatments acquittees received. For example, an acquittee who underwent mandated outpatient substance abuse treatment and was not arrested would appear less recidivistic than an untreated acquittee who was re-arrested. However, the cause of the individual's abstention from crime would be unclear. Are dispositional, clinical, treatment utilization or community factors primarily responsible for the pro-social behavior? By studying the treatments acquittees receive, one could not only reduce potential confounds but also clarify the differential efficacies of varying clinical modalities.

An additional potential confound is the evolution of the insanity statute in Illinois during the course of this study. On 1 January, 1994, the volitional component of the Illinois insanity defense was omitted. During the next four years, a public debate ensued that left the defense in somewhat of a transitory state. By late 1998, the new version of the defense was widely accepted and implemented. Therefore, persons acquitted before this period may have met different criteria than persons acquitted after the modification. In other words, the construct validity of the study may be somewhat limited.

Future Research

Researchers studying NGRI criminal recidivism must grapple with a variety of challenges: shifting legal codes; fragmented data systems; and large bureaucratic entities. These qualities and others make seemingly simple issues remarkably complex. In the midst of the confusion created by this complexity, six trends can begin to bring cohesion and clarity to the research. The following section is a discussion of these trends.

The Study of Time as an Outcome

The role of time in NGRI criminal recidivism is multifaceted and yet often neglected. There appears to be a broad linear relationship between the length of the follow up period and the rate of recidivism. However, when examined more precisely, the slope of the line appears to shift subtly over time with no clearly defined ceiling effect.[145]

In most NGRI recidivism studies, the proportion of acquittees who recidivate and the length of the follow up period are presented as the primary results. For example, Pantle and colleagues make the following statement in their 1980 study: "Of the 37 NGRI subjects out of hospital, nine (24%) incurred subsequent arrests" (p.313). Such statements communicate important information and are standard within the literature; however, they leave the following questions unanswered: Were the subjects at risk for re-offending during the entirety of the follow-up period or were there periods of time during which they were not at risk (e.g. during hospitalizations)? How much time typically passes before the first re-arrest occurs? Are there periods of time when subjects were particularly likely to recidivate (e.g. during the first year after release)? These questions and others highlight the complex role that time plays in developing a more sophisticated understanding of recidivism patterns. In a chapter addressing innovative statistical techniques in psychological research, Willett and Singer (1991) elucidate the ways in which survival analysis can help researchers answer the previous questions. The following section is a synopsis of their work and an introduction to survival analysis.

Willet and Singer identify two domains of research for which survival analysis can be particularly effective. First, clinicians and administrators often want to know how much time will pass before a particular event will occur. For example, they may want to know the mean duration between discharge and re-arrest for a group of NGRI acquittees. Second, they often want to understand the association between duration and various predictors. This latter domain concerns the variation in duration as a function of different sets of predictors. For example, do female acquittees tend to recidivate more rapidly but less frequently than males?

One of the most challenging issues for researchers studying recidivism rates is deciding what to do with those subjects who do not recidivate during the study period. For example, some acquittees will not be arrested during the time period in which they are being followed. Therefore, it is unclear how much time could pass before they would recidivate. A subject may commit an offense immediately after the end of the follow-up period, or perhaps, not recidivate even if the follow-up period were extended indefinitely.

The "censored duration" of these indeterminate cases poses a particularly vexing problem for researchers. If one wishes to determine the mean length of time before an event occurs, what duration does one enter for these cases? For example, one could enter the maximum length of the follow-up period for the censored durations; however, such a strategy assumes that these subjects would recidivate on the final day of the follow-up period. Therefore, one's results would be positively biased. Alternatively, one could simply eliminate these cases from one's calculations. Such a strategy would eliminate the upper end of the range and therefore produce negatively biased results.

Survival analysis is a statistical technique that incorporates both censored and uncensored cases into a unitary analysis.[146] Rather than assessing time directly as duration, this technique allows one to transform duration into two mathematical functions relevant both to censored and uncensored cases: the survivor and hazard functions. These functions allow researchers to conduct meaningful analyses without losing pertinent information (e.g. censored cases), and yet they produce data that can be converted back into the original functions of duration once the analyses have been completed.

The survivor function is a graphic display of the probability of not experiencing a particular event plotted against time. It is often summarized in the form of a median lifetime statistic.[147] This value is intuitively meaningful in that it represents the amount of time before half of the group has experienced a particular event (e.g. re-arrest). The hazard function allows one to identify periods of time when subjects are particularly at risk.

Willet and Singer identify the following six advantages to using these strategies over traditional analyses of duration:

- They allow one to analyze several effects simultaneously while isolating individual effects.

- They include both continuous and categorical variables as predictors.

- They allow one to study both main and interaction effects in a manner similar to linear regression models.

- Once a model has been fitted, it can be used to summarize and display the results (e.g. median lifetime statistic).

- They include variables whose values change over time.

- The effect of a predictor that varies over time can be assessed.

Inclusion of Broader Clinical Material

The clinical material included in recidivism studies has been unnecessarily limited.[148] Researchers commonly include diagnoses or isolated clinical factors (e.g. command hallucinations) as variables. However, other realms of clinical research have broadened the boundaries of clinically relevant material. For example, in the present study, numerous caregiver and environmental variables demonstrated predictive power. Prior studies support these results and suggest that factors such as financial support and housing may influence re-arrest rates.[149]

As the broader social service delivery system becomes increasingly community based, it is not prudent to focus exclusively on disturbances within individuals. Rather, the interpersonal, communal factors that lead individuals to develop particular strengths and vulnerabilities, and the ways in which individuals tend to communicate their distress to others, should be studied in concert.[150] The present study demonstrates how broader clinical material can produce more effective interventions and more powerful predictive tools.

Individualized Assessments of Risk

As change over time is studied in more sophisticated ways and broader clinical material is incorporated into conditional release programs, individualized assessments of risk can be conducted. Clinicians can move beyond the broad predictive factors, such as prior criminal history and substance use, in order to identify situations, time-tables, and patterns specific to the individuals being monitored. Hooper and colleagues (2005) refer to this approach in describing the Alabama Structured Assessment of Treatment Completion for Insanity Acquittees. They claim that "by measuring the patient's change against his own patterns [they] focus on boundaries and not simply static issues" (p. 607).[151]

Such dynamism enables clinicians to make use of comprehensive histories. For example, Haggard-Grann and Gumpert (2005) suggest that most individuals communicate their sense of distress during times of elevated risk. Both the challenge and opportunity stem from the uniqueness of the communications. In other words, although individuals often communicate in ways that are different from others, they tend to be consistent over time. Therefore, once a thorough history of an individual's communication patterns is established, clinicians can tailor their responses accordingly.

Individualized assessments of risk also involve organizing acquittees according to diagnostic subsets. For example, given our evolving understanding of post-partum psychosis, the time surrounding and following childbirth should be considered high-risk.[152] Given the influence of PTSD on criminal recidivism, clinicians can anticipate that media coverage of combat will provoke veterans.[153] Attention to clinical subsets allows staff to be increasingly flexible and responsive.

Assessing the Durability of Our Interventions
Though conditional release programs appear to be effective to varying degrees, it is unclear whether they continue to help acquittees after the release mandate ends. Bloom and colleagues (1986) suggest that the durability of these interventions is poorly understood. They found that acquittees were almost two times more likely to be re-arrested after completing the conditional release program than while participating within it. Perhaps, there is a

threshold that needs to be reached before the effects of an intervention become durable. Perhaps, conditional release programs simply have little impact on acquittees once they have completed their mandates. If the latter hypothesis is true, then alternative, more enduring means of engaging acquittees are recommended. However, until further research is conducted, it remains difficult to design adequate interventions.

Assessing Treatment Pathways
One would obviously expect that the treatments acquittees receive influence their likelihood to recidivate. Along with including broader clinical material in recidivism studies, treatment factors should shape NGRI research. For example, it will be important to know whether persons participating in dual diagnosis groups commit crimes less than individuals in standard groups. Similarly, as service pathways are modified in response to growing research findings, the need to study the impact of the interventions will become even more pressing. Over time, a feedback system could be developed that would allow researchers to monitor the impact of attempts at improvement.

The study of treatment pathways will enable comparisons of conditional release programs. At the present time, it seems at though the Oregon system is the most effective and progressive. The strength of the program seems partially due to the legal statutes and procedures surrounding the defense. For example, as opposed to many states in which the insanity defense is barely ever used presumably because their release standards are so conservative, Oregon has a larger pool of individuals successfully using the defense. If these increased numbers were correlated with excess criminal recidivism, the standards would be considered overly permissive. However, these acquittees seem to be managed in the community relatively safely. A series of factors most likely accounts for the success of the Oregon program. Not only felons but also misdemeanants can use the defense. Acquittees are given an "insanity sentence" that limits the amount of time they can be held under the jurisdiction of the PSRB. Formal consideration is given to the waxing and waning of illnesses in remission. Lastly, monitoring and treatment are integrated under the auspices of the PSRB and rapid revocation procedures are available. If an understanding of these factors were paired with better data concerning the impact of community interventions (e.g.. dual diagnosis programs, social rehabilitative centers, and vocational development services), more sophisticated and effective conditional release programs could be developed.

The Relationship between Hospital and Criminal Recidivism

The possibility that hospitalization can serve to prevent re-arrest demands further study. If the data support this claim, then conditional release programs should offer efficient revocation procedures that would allow for frequent and rapid hospitalizations when necessary. The cost of providing such services would be offset by savings gained from having more acquittees released into the community. Furthermore, they would promote patient stability, protect members of the community, and presumably reduce criminal justice costs.

Conclusion

In order to treat NGRI acquittees, clinicians and administrators must provide services in the least restrictive settings possible while also reducing the likelihood of future violence. Given the emotionally charged attitudes most people display toward insanity acquittees, this balance has often been inordinately influenced by shifts in public opinion.[154] We need reliable data in order to balance individual freedoms with public safety, and safeguard us from our own biases. Past studies have provided a sound and yet somewhat disjointed foundation upon which to build service delivery systems. It now seems worthwhile to study the treatment pathways we have established in order to assess their efficacy.

By broadening the clinical material we collect, treating time as a complex and multifaceted factor, and assessing the durability of our interventions, we can develop a more sophisticated understanding of recidivism patterns and clinical progress among NGRI acquittees. Actuarial data can be integrated with broad clinical material to improve clinical outcomes and reduce post-discharge recidivism. The goal of such innovations is to develop models that allow clinicians and administrators to match clients with service pathways that account for varying levels of risk and clinical need. Once such a structure is in place, it will be possible to track the movement of subjects through the system in order to assess the efficacy of specific pathways and the appropriateness of pathway-client matches.

Given the relatively small number of insanity acquittees, efforts to study their service delivery systems may seem misguided. However, their broader relevance stems partially from the liminal position they hold between the mental health and criminal justice systems. By learning about insanity acquittees, we learn about mentally ill persons in our criminal justice system and criminally involved individuals in our psychiatric hospitals. Given that roughly 1 out of every 138 persons in the United States in 2004 was in prison or jail and that roughly 16% of these people have mental illnesses, improved programs for integrating mentally ill, criminally involved people into the community would have a profound impact. Where mental illness and crime intersect, emotions flair, the social and the personal overlap, and clinicians, researchers, and administrators often become confused and reactive. For these reasons, informed, thoughtful perspectives hold particular promise.

---

[132]Bloom et al, 1986; Pasewark et al, 1979.

[133]Cirincione et al, 1995.

[134]Bellak, A., & Gearon, J. (2002). Substance abuse treatment for people with schizophrenia. *Addictive Behaviors*, 23(6), 749-766; Grella, C., & Gilmore, J. (2002). Improving service delivery to the dually diagnosed in Los Angeles County. *Journal of Substance Abuse Treatment*, 23(2), 115-122; Timko, C., & Moos, R. (2002). Symptom severity, amount of treatment and 1-year outcomes among dual diagnosis patients. *Administration and Policy in Mental Health*, 30(1), 35-54.

[135]Liu, H. (1997). Burnout and organizational commitment among staff of publicly funded substance abuse treatment programs. *Dissertation Abstracts*, 58(6A), 2386; Walko, S., Pratt, C., Siiter, R., & Ellison, K. (1993). Predicting staff retention in psychiatric rehabilitation. *Psychosocial Rehabilitation Journal*, 16(3), 150-153.

[136]Farabee, D., Shen, H., & Sanchez, S. (2002). Perceived coercion and treatment need among mentally ill parolees. *Criminal Justice and Behavior*, 29(1), 76-86; Silverberg, J., Vital, T., & Brakel, S. (2001). Breaking down barriers to mandated outpatient treatment for mentally ill offenders. *Psychiatric Annals*, 31(7), 433-440.

[137]Lamb et al, 1989.

[138]Sellwood, W., Barrowclough, C., Tarrier, N., Quinn, J., Mainwaring, J., & Lewis, S. (2002). Needs-based cognitive-behavioral family

intervention for carers of patients suffering from schizophrenia: 12 month follow-up. *Acta Psychiatrica Scandinavica*, 104(5), 346-355.

[139]Walker, E. (2000). Spiritual support in relation to community violence exposure, aggressive outcomes, and psychological adjustment among inner-city young adolescents. *Dissertation Abstracts*, 61(6B), 3295.

[140]Greene, G. J., Lee, M, Trask, R., & Rheinscheld, J. (2005). How to word with clients' strengths in crisis intervention: A solution-focused approach. In A. Roberts (Ed.), *Crisis intervention handbook: Assessment, treatment, and research*, 3rd ed. (pp. 64-89). New York: Oxford University Press.

[141]Goethe, J., Dornelas, E., & Fischer, E. (1996). A cluster analytic study of functional outcome after psychiatric hospitalization. *Comprehensive Psychiatry*, 37(2), 115-121.

[142]Di Masso, J., Avi-Itzhak, T., & Obler, D. R. (2001). The clubhouse model: An outcome study on attendance, work attainment and status, and hospitalization recidivism. *Work*, 17(1), 23-30.

[143]Chou, K., Liu, S., & Chu, H. (2002). The effects of support groups on caregivers of patients with schizophrenia. *International Journal of Nursing Studies*, 39(7), 713-722.

[144]Hooper, J. F., McLearen, A. M., & Barnett, M. E. (2005). The Alabama Structured Assessment of Treatment Completion for Insanity Acquittes (The AlaSATcom). *International Journal of Law and Psychiatry*, 28(6), 604-612; Teplin, 1994.

[145]Harris, 2000.

[146]Willett, J. B. & Singer, J. D. (1991). How long did it take? Using survival analysis in educational and psychological research. In L. M. Collins & J. L. Horn (Eds), *Best methods for the analysis of change: Recent advances, unanswered questions, future directions (pp. 310-327)*. Washington, DC: American Psychological Association.

[147]Ibid.

[148]Haggard-Grann, U. & Gumpert, C. (2005). The violence relapse process – a qualitative analysis of high-risk situations and risk communication in mentally disordered offenders. *Psychology, Crime & Law*, 11(2), 199-222.

[149]Ibid; Harris, 2000; Feder, L. (1991). A comparison of the community adjustment of mentally ill offenders with those from the general prison population: An 18-month follow-up. *Law and Human Behavior*, 15(5), 477-493; Jemelka, R. P., Trupin, E., & Chiles, J. A. The mentally ill in prison: A review. Hospital and Community Psychiatry, 40, 481-491.

[150]Haggard-Grann & Gumpert, 2005.

[151]Brown, K. (2003). *Presentation to the 2003 NASMHPD Meeting*, Little Rock, Arkansas.

[152]Friedman, S. H., Hrouda, D. R., Holden, C. E., Noffsinger, S. G., & Resnick, P. J. (2005). Child murder committed by severely mentally ill mothers: An examination of mothers found not guilty by reason of insanity. *Journal of Forensic Science*, 50(6), 1466-71.

[153]Kubiak, S. P. (2004). The effects of PTSD on treatment adherence, drug relapse, and criminal recidivism in a sample of incarcerated men and women. *Research on Social Work Practice*, 14(6), 424-433.

[154]Perlin, 1996.

NGRI Research Programs

California: Lamb and colleagues (1988) followed 79 NGRI acquittees in California for an average of 3.8 years. Each of the acquittees was participating in California's conditional release program that had been modeled on the programs used in Oregon, Illinois and Maryland. Of the 79 subjects, 25 acquittees (31.6%) were re-arrested at least once during the follow up period. Eighteen of these persons (22.8%) were arrested specifically for violent crimes. The researchers organized the subjects according to three categories: those individuals who remained in mandated outpatient treatment during the entirety of the follow up period; those persons who had been released from treatment either because jurisdiction expired or they were deemed no longer dangerously mentally ill; and those persons who had their release revoked and then were never returned to a treatment program after being subsequently released. The first group, who had remained in treatment through the duration of the follow up period, had the lowest rate of violent recidivism and hospitalization. The third group, whose released had been revoked and then reinstated without treatment, had the most subsequent arrests and hospitalizations. Through a qualitative review of the records, the researchers determined that the third group had been given adequate supervision and structure during the original treatment period.

Canada: Luettgen and colleagues (1998) followed 74 Canadian NGRI acquittees for 6.7 years on average (mean). They tracked convictions rather than arrests. Eight of these individuals (10.8%) were convicted of 25 post-discharge crimes. Only 2 of the 74 acquittees (2.7%) were convicted for a violent crime. The researchers translated these data into yearly re-offense rates and found that the acquittees' overall rate of violent recidivism (1.8%) did not differ significantly from the general Canadian population's rate (1.0%). They identified five correlates to re-conviction: male, younger, prior convictions, schizophrenia and/or comorbid substance dependence/abuse.

Hawaii: Bogenberger and colleagues (1987) followed 107 Hawaiian NGRI acquittees between 8 and 14.5 years. As would be expected from a study in Hawaii, the sample resembled other NGRI samples except there were more persons of Filipino, Japanese, Chinese and Hawaiian descent. Seventy-two of the 107 subjects (67.3%) accumulated 362 arrests. Nearly 17% of the post-acquittal arrests compared with 52% of pre-acquittal arrests, were for crimes against persons. The method of measuring the proportion of violent arrests rather than the proportion of individuals arrested for violent crimes again possess problems for comparisons across studies. The elevation in the recidivism rate may be due to the extended follow up period. Only three other studies (Spodak et al., 1984; Silver et al., & Kravitz et al., 1999) used comparable follow up periods. Even though the rate of criminal recidivism was high, the severity of the crimes committed appears to diminish over time. Those persons who had been hospitalized post-acquittal accounted for the largest proportion of "serious crimes" (combined categories of crimes against persons and property v. combined categories of public order and drug offenses).

Illinois: Cavanaugh and Wasyliw (1985) followed a group of 44 NGRI acquittees participating in a conditional release program in Illinois. They followed the subjects between 1 and 2 years. Though two of the acquittees (4.5%) were re-arrested, neither committed a violent crime. The acquittees were more than five times as likely to be re-hospitalized (25%) than re-arrested (4.5%). Perhaps, as others have suggested previously, hospitalization is an effective tool for preventing criminal recidivism (citations). The therapists responsible for mandating the hospitalizations reported that every subject who was hospitalized either had stopped taken psychotropic medications or had begun abusing alcohol or other drugs. Given the low rate of criminal recidivism, no correlates of re-arrest were identified.

The most recent study was conducted by Kravitz and colleagues in IL (1999). They followed 43 acquittees for 4.9-18.4 years (mean = 5.75 years). Eight of the 43 subjects (18.6%) were re-arrested, and 5 (11.6%) were re-arrested for violent crimes. The following factors were linked to criminal recidivism: poor social adjustment; dependent living situation; and poor outcome after most recent psychiatric episode. The study is valuable because of its relative recency and the long follow up period.

<u>Maryland</u>: Spodak and colleagues (1984) published results concerning 86 NGRI acquittees in Maryland. They followed these subjects between 5 and 15 years (Mean = 9.5 years). By using a longer follow-up period, the authors were able to study the acquittees both during and after conditional release. Forty-eight of the 86 subjects (55.8%) were re-arrested and 12 subjects (14.0%) were re-arrested for violent crimes. Most of the criminal charges occurred within the first five years after discharge from the hospital (during the conditional release period) and 47% of the charges resulted in convictions. In all but three cases, the post-release offense posed less danger than the index offense. Those individuals who had not been hospitalized, but rather sent immediately into the conditional release program, appeared to be at greatest risk.

Silver and colleagues (1989) followed 127 Maryland NGRI acquittees for a time period ranging from 7-17 years (mean = 10.5 years). A random sample of prison parolees served as a control group and a matched sample of prison parolees who had received mental health treatment before discharge served as a comparison group. Re-arrest rates were calculated at three different time intervals: 2.5, 5, and 17 years. The mentally disordered parolees were re-arrested more often than the NGRI and control groups. Their crimes were more serious and the time until their first post-release arrest was shorter. The NGRI and control groups consistently had comparable rates. The NGRI acquittee re-arrest rates were as follows: 43/127 (33.8%) at 2 years; 69/127 (54.3%) at 5 years; and 83/127 (65.8%) at 17 years.

<u>Missouri</u>: In 1966, Morrow and Peterson published a study of 35 male NGRI acquittees released within Missouri. They compared these subjects with a group of criminal sexual psychopaths and a group of discharged prisoners from a large Federal sample. The subjects were followed for up to six years. Three year cumulative conviction rates were calculated. Since being released, 13 of the 35 NGRI acquittees (37.1%) were convicted of a felony crime and 2 acquittees (5.7%) were convicted of an assaultive felony offense. Two factors were associated with failures (defined as either re-hospitalization or conviction for a felony offense): multiple convictions (including index and prior charges) for "economic offenses;" and/or prior felony conviction. Violent recidivism within this group was comparable to rates within the randomly sampled prison group. The majority of subsequent studies used arrest rather than conviction rates, and incorporated both misdemeanor and felony charges into rate calculations. Therefore, one

would expect the rates found by Morrow and colleagues to be lower than subsequent arrest rates. As will be demonstrated, the results from subsequent studies do not consistently support this expectation.

Ohio: In the first and only NGRI criminal recidivism study in Ohio, Stafford and Karpawich (1997) followed 38 acquittees participating in a conditional release program. The follow up period is not specified clearly. Five of these acquittees (13.2%) were re-arrested. None had committed felony offenses. Though the conditional release program is discussed in depth, the authors do not describe the characteristics of the acquittees.

Oklahoma: Within the 1990s, five studies addressed violent recidivism among NGRI acquittees. In the first study, Nicholson and colleagues (1991) followed 33 NGRI acquittees from Oklahoma for 2.75 years on average (mean). Ten of the 30 acquittees (33.3%) were arrested after entering the community. The researchers divided the NGRI group into three subgroups: acquittees who went AWOL (n = 5); acquittees who were released after being treated in the forensic unit (n = 16); and acquittees who were released at the first court review (n = 9). The acquittees who went AWOL had the highest rate of re-arrest (80.0%), the untreated group was second (33.3%), and the treated group was the least recidivistic (18.8%).

Oregon: Within Oregon, Rogers and colleagues (1982) followed 165 NGRI acquittees under the supervision of the Psychiatric Security Review Board (PSRB) during a three year period. The PSRB has served as a model for similar entities in Connecticut, Utah, Kentucky and Florida (Bloom and colleagues, 1991). An academic research team is integrated into the structure of the PSRB making data collection easier. In studying recidivism, researchers collect data on the number of "crimes charged" after release. It is unclear what exactly "crimes charged" means in the present context. Perhaps, the recidivistic acquittees are arrested and held, arraigned and indicted, or possibly even convicted. Given the ambiguity, it is difficult to locate this study on the spectrum of definitions of recidivism ranging from police contact to conviction. Seventeen of the 165 subjects (10.3%) were re-charged for a crime and 8 of the 165 subjects (4.8%) were re-charged specifically for a violent crime. No data were given to differentiate the recidivistic acquittees from the non-recidivistic subjects.

In an additional study in Oregon, Rogers and colleagues (1984) followed 295 NGRI acquittees for a time period ranging from 14 to 61 months. They found that 39 of the subjects (13.2%) were re-charged and 15 subjects (5.1%) were re-charged for a violent crime. Recidivism was not associated with any demographic or clinical factors. Bloom and colleagues (1986) further examined the efficacy of the Oregon PSRB by following 67 NGRI acquittees for 2 years. Eleven of the acquittees (16.4%) were re-arrested for crimes rated less serious than the index crimes. Though no correlates of recidivism were identified, the authors reported that they had repeatedly witnessed a connection between cognitive impairment and criminal activity through their clinical work.

Bloom and colleagues (1986) conducted an additional study in Oregon with a larger sample of NGRI acquittees. They followed 123 acquittees for no more than three years. Their study is unique in that they monitored police contacts rather than arrests or convictions. They found that 31 subjects (25.2%) had contact with the police while under the supervision of the PSRB whereas 53 acquittees (43.0%) had police contact after being discharged from the conditional release program. In addition, they compared rates of criminal recidivism (as measure by police contact) among persons discharged from the conditional release program because PSRB jurisdiction expired with those acquittees released because the committee deemed them no longer dangerously mentally ill. Though persons who had police contacts while under supervision from the program were less likely to be released through committee decision (rather than jurisdiction expiration), they were comparably likely to have police contact after discharge. When considering all of the acquittees, younger age and prior arrest history were correlated with post-discharge police contact.

Adult Needs and Strengths Assessment

Problem Presentation

Psychosis

This item is used to rate symptoms of psychiatric disorders with a known neurological base. DSM-IV disorders included on this dimension are Schizophrenia and Psychotic disorders (unipolar, bipolar, NOS). The common symptoms of these disorders include hallucinations, delusions, unusual thought processes, strange speech, and bizarre/idiosyncratic behavior.

0   This level indicates an individual with no evidence of thought disturbances. Both thought processes and content are within normal range.

1   This rating indicates an individual with evidence of mild disruption in thought processes or content. The individual may be somewhat tangential in speech or evidence somewhat illogical thinking. This also includes persons with a history of hallucinations but none currently. The category would be used for individuals who are below the threshold for one of the DSM diagnoses listed above.

2   This rating indicates an individual with evidence of moderate disturbance in thought process or content. The individual may be somewhat delusional or have brief or intermittent hallucinations. The person's speech may be at times quite tangential or illogical. This level would be used for individuals who meet the diagnostic criteria for one of the disorders listed above.

3   This rating indicates an individual with severe psychotic disorder. The individual frequently is experiencing symptoms of psychosis and frequently has no reality assessment. There is evidence of ongoing delusions or hallucinations or both. Command hallucinations would be coded here. This level is used for extreme cases of the diagnoses listed above.

Impulse Control

Symptoms of Impulse Control problems that might occur in a number of disorders including Intermittent Explosive Disorder or Borderline Personality Disorder would be rated here.

0   This rating is used to indicate an individual with no evidence of impulse problems. Individual is able to regulate and self-manage behavior and affect.

1   This rating is used to indicate an individual with evidence of mild problems with impulse control problems. An individual may have some difficulties with sitting still or paying attention or may occasionally engage in impulsive behavior.

2   This rating is used to indicate an individual with moderate impulse control problems. An individual who meets DSM-IV diagnostic criteria for impulse control disorder would be rated here. Persons who use poor judgment or put themselves in jeopardy would be rated here (e.g., picking fights).

3   This rating is used to indicate an individual with severe impulse control. Frequent impulsive behavior is observed or noted that carries considerable safety risk (e.g., running into the street and dangerous driving).

Depression/Anxiety

Symptoms included in this dimension are depressed mood, social withdrawal, anxious mood, sleep disturbances, weight/eating disturbances, and loss of motivation. This dimension can be used to rate symptoms of the following psychiatric disorders as specified in DSM-IV: Depression (unipolar, dysthymia, NOS), Bipolar, Generalized Anxiety, and Phobias.

0   This rating is given to an individual with no emotional problems. No evidence of depression or anxiety.

1   This rating is given to an individual with mild emotional problems. Brief duration of depression, irritability, or impairment of peer, family, vocational or academic function that does not lead to gross avoidance behavior. This level is used to rate either a mild phobia or anxiety problem or a level of symptoms that is below the threshold for the other listed disorders.

2   This rating is given to an individual with a moderate level of emotional disturbance. This could include major conversion symptoms, frequent anxiety attacks, obsessive rituals, flashbacks, hypervigilance, depression, or school/work avoidance. This level is used to rate individuals who meet the criteria for an affective disorder as listed above.

3   This rating is given to an individual with a severe level of emotional disturbance. This would include a person who stays at home or in bed all day due to anxiety or depression or whose emotional symptoms prevent any participation in school/work, social settings, or family life. More severe forms of anxiety or depressive diagnoses would be coded here. This level is used to indicate an extreme case of one of the disorders listed above.

Antisocial Behavior

These symptoms include antisocial behaviors like shoplifting, lying, vandalism, cruelty to animals, and assault.

0   This rating indicates an individual with no evidence of antisocial disorder.

1   This rating indicates an individual with a mild level of conduct problems.   Some difficulties in school/work and home behavior.   Problems recognizable but not notably deviant. This might include occasional lying or petty theft from family.

2   This rating indicates an individual with a moderate level of conduct disorder.   This could include episodes of planned aggression or other antisocial behavior.

3   This rating indicates an individual with a severe Conduct Disorder.   This could include frequent episodes of unprovoked, planned aggression or other antisocial behavior.

Substance Abuse

These symptoms include use of alcohol and illegal drugs, the misuse of prescription medications and the inhalation of any substance for recreational purposes.   This dimension is rated consistent with DSM-IV Substance Related Disorders.

0   This rating is for an individual who has no notable substance use difficulties at the present time.   If the person is in recovery for greater than 1 year they should be coded here.

1   This rating is for an individual with mild substance use problems that might occasionally present problems of living for the person (i.e., intoxication, loss of money, and reduced work performance).   This rating would be used for someone early in recovery (less than 1 year) who is currently maintaining abstinence for at least 30 days.

2   This rating is for an individual with a moderate substance abuse problem that both requires treatment and interacts with and exacerbates the psychiatric illness. A substance abuse problem that consistently interferes with the ability to function optimally, but does not completely preclude functioning in an unstructured setting.

3   This rating is for an individual with a severe substance dependence condition that presents a significant complication to the mental health management (e.g., need for detoxification) of the individual.

Adjustment to Trauma

This rating covers the reactions of individuals to a variety of traumatic experiences. This dimension covers both adjustment disorders and post traumatic stress disorder from DSM-IV.

0   The individual has not experienced any trauma or has adjusted well to significant traumatic experiences.

1   The individual has some mild adjustment problems and exhibits some signs of distress.

2   The individual has marked adjustment problems and is symptomatic in response to a traumatic event (e.g., anger, depression, and anxiety).

3   The individual has post traumatic stress difficulties. Symptoms may include intrusive thoughts, hyper-vigilance, constant anxiety, and other common symptoms of Post Traumatic Stress Disorder (PTSD).

Personality Disorder

This rating identifies the presence of any DSM-IV Axis II personality disorder

0   No evidence of symptoms of a personality disorder.

1   Evidence of mild degree, probably sub-threshold for the diagnosis of a personality disorder. For example, mild but consistent dependency in relationships might be rated here. Or, some evidence of mild antisocial or narcissistic behavior. Also, an unconfirmed suspicion of the presence of a diagnosable personality disorder would be rated here.

2   Evidence of sufficient degree of personality disorder to warrant a DSM-IV Axis II diagnosis.

3   Evidence of a severe personality disorder that has significant implications for the individual long-term functioning. Personality disorder dramatically interferes with the individual's ability to function independently.

Problem Modifiers

Situational Consistency of Problems

This rating captures the variation in problem presentation across different situations and environments in the individual's life (e.g., work, home and school).

0   Problems generally occur in only one environment and/or situation.

1   Problems occur in multiple setting and/or situations but tend to be most severe in a single setting.

2   Problems occur in many settings and/or situations but there is variability in the severity of the problems with the individual doing better in some circumstances than in others.

3   Problems occur consistently in all situations.

Temporal Consistency of Problems

This rating captures the duration of mental health problems experienced by the individual. Include both problems (i.e., symptoms) and risk behaviors in this rating.

0   Problems began in the past six months after the occurrence of a specific stressful event.

1   Problems began more than six months but less than two years ago, or problems began in the past six months in the absence of any specific stressful event.

2   Problems began more than two years ago but the individual has had at least one period of more than one month where he/she has been relatively symptom free.

3   Problems began more than two years ago and the individual has remained fairly consistently symptomatic over this period of time.

Motivation for Care

This rating captures the desire for the individual to participate in their care. The person need not understanding their illness, however they participate in recommended or prescribed care (e.g., taking prescribed medications and attending therapy).

0   The individual cooperates and participates in all recommended or prescribed care.

1   The individual is willing to participate in care, however may need prompts at times.

2   The individual is mostly unwilling to participate in care and participates infrequently.

3   The individual refuses to participate in care including taking prescribed medications or attending therapy.

Risk Behaviors

Danger to Self

A rating of '2' or '3' would indicate the need for a safety plan.

0   No evidence or history of suicidal or self-injurious behaviors.

1   The individual has a history of suicidal or self-injurious behavior but no self-injurious behavior during the past 30 days.

2   The individual has expressed recent (last 30 days), but not acute (today) suicidal ideation or gesture. Self-injurious behavior in the past 30 days (including today) without suicidal ideation or intent.

3   Current suicidal ideation and intent in the past 24 hours.

Danger to Others

This includes actual and threatened violence. Imagined violence, when extreme, may be rated here. A rating of '2' or '3' would indicate the need for a safety plan.

0   No evidence or history of aggressive behaviors or significant verbal aggression towards others (includes people and animals).

1   A history of aggressive behavior or verbal aggression towards others but no aggression during the past 30 days. A history of fire setting (not in the past year) would be rated here.

2   Occasional or moderate level of aggression towards others including aggression during the past 30 days or more recent verbal aggression.

3   Frequent or dangerous (significant harm) level of aggression to others. Any fire setting within the past year would be rated here. The individual is an immediate risk to others.

Sexually Inappropriate Behavior

Sexually inappropriate behavior includes both aggressive sexual behavior against another individual and inappropriate sexual behavior (e.g., language and disrobing).

0   No evidence of problems with sexual behavior in the past year.

1   Mild problems of sexual behavior. For example, occasional inappropriate sexual gesturing or language.

2   Moderate problems with sexual behavior. For example, frequent inappropriate sexual gesturing or language. Frequent disrobing would be rated here only if it was sexually provocative. Frequent inappropriate touching would be rated here.

3   Severe problems with sexually abusive behavior. This would include the rape or sexual abuse of another person involving sexual penetration.

Social Behavior

This rating refers to how an individual behaves in public or social settings and should reflect problematic social behaviors (socially unacceptable behavior for the culture and community in which he/she lives) that put the individual at some risk (not excessive shyness).

0   No evidence of problematic social behaviors.

1   A mild level of problematic social behaviors. This might include occasional inappropriate social behavior. Infrequent inappropriate comments to strangers or unusual behavior in social settings might be included in this level.

2   A moderate level of problematic social behaviors. Frequent cursing in public would be rated here.

3   A severe level of problematic social behaviors. This would be indicated by frequent, seriously inappropriate social behaviors such as threatening strangers.

Crime

This rating includes both criminal behavior and status offenses that may result from the individual failing to follow required behavioral standards. This category does not include drug usage but it does include drug sales and other drug related activities. Sexual offenses should be included as criminal behavior.

0   No evidence or history of criminal or delinquent behavior.

1   A history of criminal or delinquent behavior but none in the past year. Status offenses in the past year would be rated here.

2   A moderate level of criminal activity. This level indicates a person who has been engaged in criminal activity during the past year, but the criminal activity does not represent a significant physical risk to others in the community. Examples would include vandalism and shoplifting.

3   A severe level of criminal activity. This level indicates a person who has been engaged in violent criminal activity during the past year which represent a significant physical risk to others in the community. Examples would include rape, armed robbery, and assault.

Victimization

This item is used to examine a history and level of current risk for victimization.

0   This level indicates a person with no evidence of recent victimization and no significant history of victimization within the past year. The person may have been robbed or burglarized on one or more occasions in the past, but no pattern of victimization exists. Person is not presently at risk for re-victimization.

1   This level indicates a person with a history of victimization but who has not been victimized to any significant degree in the past year.   Person is not presently at risk for re-victimization.

2   This level indicates a person who has been recently victimized (within the past year) but is not in acute risk of re-victimization.   This might include physical or sexual abuse, significant psychological abuse by family or friend, extortion or violent crime.

3   This level indicates a person who has been recently victimized and is in acute risk of re-victimization.   Examples include working as a prostitute and living in an abusive relationship.

Functioning

Intellectual Development

This rating is intended to capture a functioning problem such as low IQ, mental retardation, or other developmental disability.

0   No evidence of intellectual or developmental impairment.

1   Low IQ (i.e., 71 to 85) or mild developmental delay.

2   Mild mental retardation (i.e., 50 to 70).

3   Moderate to severe mental retardation (less than 50) or severe or Pervasive Developmental Disorder.

Knowledge of Illness

This rating is intended to capture an individual's awareness and understanding for their psychiatric symptoms and diagnosis.

0   This level indicates a person who is aware of his/her psychiatric diagnosis and can verbalize an understanding of the nature, symptoms, and course of the illness. Any person who is sub-threshold on psychiatric diagnoses would be rated here.

1   This level indicates a person who is aware that he/she has an illness but is not clear about its implications.

2   This level indicates a person who is unaware that he/she has an illness but recognizes that there is a problem.

3   This level indicates a person who refuses to accept his/her illness despite clear evidence of a psychiatric disorder.

Physical/Medical

This rating includes both health problems and chronic/acute physical conditions.

0   No evidence of physical or medical problems.

1   Mild or well-managed physical or medical problems. This might include well-managed chronic conditions like diabetes or asthma.

2   Chronic physical or moderate medical problems.

3   Severe, life threatening physical or medical conditions.

Family Functioning

The definition of family should be from the perspective of the individual (i.e., who does the individual consider to be family). Family functioning should be rated independently of the problems experienced or stimulated by the individual currently assessed.

0   No evidence of family problems.

1   A mild to moderate level of family problems including marital difficulties and problems between siblings.

2   A significant level of family problems including frequent arguments, difficult separation and/or divorce, and siblings with significant mental health, developmental or criminal justice problems.

3   A profound level of family disruption including significant criminality or domestic violence.

Employment/Educational Functioning

This rates the performance of the individual in school or work settings. This performance can include issues of behavior, attendance or achievement/productivity.

0   No evidence of behavior problems at school or work. Individual is gainfully employed or in school.

1   A mild degree of problems with school or work functioning including limited educational progress or mild behavior problems. Individual may have some problems in work environment.

2   A moderate degree of school or work problems including disruptive behavior and/or difficulties with learning. Individual may have history of frequent job loss or may be recently unemployed.

3   A severe degree of school or work problems including aggressive behavior toward teachers, peers, superiors or failure to learn. Individual is chronically unemployed and not attending any education program.

Independent Living Skills

This rating focuses on the presence or absence of short or long-term risks associated with impairments in independent living abilities.

0   This level indicates a person who is fully capable of independent living. No evidence of any deficits that could impede maintaining own home.

1   This level indicates a person with mild impairment of independent living skills. Some problems exist with maintaining reasonable cleanliness, diet and so forth. Problems with money management may occur at this level. These problems are generally addressable with training or supervision.

2   This level indicates a person with moderate impairment of independent living skills. Notable problems with completing tasks necessary for independent living are apparent. Difficulty with cooking, cleaning, and self-management when unsupervised would be common at this level. Problems are generally addressable with in-home services.

3   This level indicates a person with profound impairment of independent living skills. This individual would be expected to be unable to live independently given their current status. Problems require a structured living environment.

Residential Stability

This item is used to rate the caregiver's current and likely future housing circumstances for the individual. If the individual lives independently, their history of residential stability can be rated.

0   There is no evidence of residential instability. The caregiver(s) has stable housing for the foreseeable future.

1   The caregiver(s) has relatively stable housing but has either moved in the past three months or there are indications that housing problems could arise at some point within the next three months. Also, a mild degree of residential instability if living independently, characterized by the potential loss of housing due to the person's difficulty with self-care, disruptive behavior, financial situation, or other psychosocial stressor. A recent move for any reason that the individual found stressful would be rated here.

2   The caregiver(s) has moved multiple times in the past year. Also, a moderate degree of residential instability if the person is living independently, characterized by recent and temporary lack of permanent housing.

3   The caregiver(s) has experienced periods of homelessness in the past six months. Also, significant degree of residential instability if living independently, characterized by homelessness for at least 30 days as defined by living on the streets, in shelters, or other transitional housing.

Care Intensity and Organization

Monitoring

This item is used to rate the level of monitoring needed to address the safety and functioning needs of the individual.

0   The individual has minimal monitoring needs.

1   The individual has some monitoring needs. For example, a caregiver would need to check on the individual during awake hours but not during asleep hours.

2   The individual has significant monitoring needs. For example, a caregiver would need to be in the same room or nearby most of the time during awake hours and nearby during asleep hours.

3   The individual needs 24-hour awake monitoring.

Treatment

This item is used to rate the intensity of the treatment needed to address the problems, risk behaviors, and functioning of the individual.

0   The individual has no behavioral, physical, or medical treatment needs.

1   The individual requires weekly behavioral, physical, or medical treatment.

2   The individual requires daily behavioral, physical, or medical treatment. This would include ensuring that the individual takes daily medication.

3   The individual requires multiple and complex daily behavioral, physical, and medical treatments.

Transportation

This item is used to rate the level of transportation required to ensure that the individual could effectively participate in his/her own treatment.

0   The individual has no transportation needs.

1   The individual has occasional transportation needs (e.g., appointments). These needs would be no more than weekly and not require a special vehicle.

2   The individual has occasional transportation needs that require a special vehicle or frequent transportation needs (e.g., daily to work or therapy) that do not require a special vehicle.

3   The individual requires frequent (e.g., daily to work or therapy) transportation in a special vehicle.

Service Permanence

This item is used to rate the stability of the service providers who have worked with the individual or family.

0   Service providers have been consistent for more than the past two years. This level also is used to rate an individual/family who is initiating services for the first time or re-initiating services after an absence from services of at least one year.

1   Service providers have been consistent for at least one year, but changes occurred during the prior year.

2   Service providers have been changed recently after a period of consistency.

3   Service providers have changed multiple times during the past year.

Self-Care

This rating focuses on current status of self-care functioning.

0   No evidence of self-care impairments. This is characterized by the ability to independently complete all activities of daily living such as bathing, grooming, dressing, cooking, and managing personal finances.

1   A mild degree of impairment with self-care. This is characterized by self-care difficulties that impair the individual's level of functioning, but do not represent a significant short or long-term threat to the person's well-being.

2   A moderate degree of self-care impairment. This is characterized by an extreme disruption in one self-care skill or moderate disruption in more than one self-care skill. The person's self-care does not represent an immediate threat to the person's safety but has the potential for creating significant long-term problems if not addressed.

3   A significant degree of self-care impairment. This is characterized by extreme disruptions in multiple self-care skills. The person's self-care abilities are sufficiently impaired that he/she represents an immediate threat to himself/herself and requires 24-hour supervision to ensure safety. (Suicidal or homicidal ideation or behavior would not be coded here, however, an acute eating disorder would be coded here).

Medication Compliance

This rating focuses on the level of the individual's willingness and participation in taking prescribed medications.

0   This level indicates a person who takes psychotropic medications as prescribed and without reminders, or a person who is not currently on any psychotropic medication.

1   This level indicates a person who will take psychotropic medications routinely, but who sometimes needs reminders to maintain compliance.   Also, a history of medication noncompliance but no current problems would be rated here.

2   This level indicates a person who is somewhat non-compliant. This person may be resistant to taking psychotropic medications or this person may tend to overuse his or her medications.   He/she might comply with prescription plans for periods of time (1-2 weeks) but generally does not sustain taking medication in prescribed dose or protocol.

3   This level indicates a person who has refused to take prescribed psychotropic medications during the past 30 day period or a person who has abused his or her medications to a significant degree (i.e., overdosing or over using medications to a dangerous degree).

Family/Caregiver Capacity

Caregiver refers to parent(s) or other adult with primary care-taking responsibilities for the individual.   This dimension would not be applicable to an individual living in an institutionalized setting, however would apply to someone living in group homes.

Physical/Behavioral Health

Physical and Behavioral Health includes medical, physical, mental health, and substance abuse challenges faced by the caregiver(s).

0   The caregiver(s) has no physical or behavioral health limitations that impact assistance or attendant care.

1   The caregiver(s) has some physical or behavioral health limitations that interfere with provision of assistance or attendant care.

2   The caregiver(s) has significant physical or behavioral health limitations that prevent them from being able to provide some needed assistance or that make attendant care difficult.

3   The caregiver(s) is unable to provide any needed assistance or attendant care.

Involvement with Care

This item is used to rate the level of involvement the caregiver(s) has in the planning and provision of mental health related services.

0   This level indicates a caregiver(s) who is actively involved in the planning and/or implementation of services and is able to be an effective advocate on behalf of the individual.

1   This level indicates a caregiver(s) who is consistently involved in the planning and/or implementation of services for the individual but is not an active advocate on their behalf.

2   This level indicates a caregiver(s) who is minimally involved in the care of the individual. Caregiver(s) may visit the individual when living in an out-of-home placement, but does not become involved in service planning and implementation.

3   This level indicates a caregiver(s) who is uninvolved with the care of the individual. The caregiver(s) may want the individual out of home or fails to visit the individual when in residential placement.

Knowledge

This item is used to rate the caregiver's knowledge of the specific strengths of the individual and any problems experienced by the individual and their ability to understand the rationale for the treatment or management of these problems.

0   This level indicates that the present caregiver(s) is fully knowledgeable about the individual's psychological strengths and weaknesses, talents, and limitations.

1   This level indicates that the present caregiver(s), while being generally knowledgeable about the individual, has some mild deficits in knowledge or understanding of either the person's psychological condition or his/her talents, skills, and assets.

2   This level indicates that the caregiver(s) does not know or understand the individual well and that significant deficits exist in the caregiver's ability to relate to the person's problems and strengths.

3   This level indicates that the present caregiver(s) has little or no understanding of the individual's current condition. The caregiver(s) is unable to cope with the individual given his/her status at the time, not because of the needs of the person but because the caregiver(s) does not understand or accept the situation.

Resources

This item is used to refer to the financial and social assets (extended family) and resources that the caregiver(s) can bring to bear in addressing the multiple needs of the individual and family.

0   The caregiver(s) has sufficient resources so that there are few limitations on what can be provided for the individual.

1   The caregiver(s) has the necessary resources to help address the individual's major and basic needs, but those resources might be stretched.

2   The caregiver(s) has limited resources (e.g., a relative living in the same town who is sometimes available to assist with the individual).

3   The caregiver(s) has severely limited resources that are available to assist in the care and treatment of the individual.

Organization

This rating should be based on the ability of the caregiver(s) to participate in or direct the organization of the household, services, and related activities.

0   The caregiver(s) is well organized and efficient.

1   The caregiver(s) has minimal difficulties with organizing or maintaining the household to support needed services. For example, the caregiver(s) may be forgetful about appointments or occasionally fails to call back the case manager.

2   The caregiver(s) has moderate difficulty organizing or maintaining the household to support needed services.

3   The caregiver(s) is unable to organize the household to support needed services.

Safety

This item is used to refer to the safety of the assessed individual. It does not refer to the safety of other family or household members. The presence of an individual (family or stranger) that presents a safety risk to the individual should be rated. This item does not refer to the safety of the physical environment in which the individual lives (e.g., a broken or loose staircase).

0   This rating indicates that the current placement presents no risk to the safety of the individual in his/her present condition.

1   This rating indicates that the current placement presents some mild risk of neglect or exposure to drug use, but that no immediate risk is present.

2   This rating indicates that there is risk to the individual including such things as the risk of abuse or exposure to individuals who could harm the individual.

3   This rating indicates that the current placement presents a significant risk to the well-being of the individual. Risk of harm is imminent and immediate.

Strengths

Family

All family members with whom the individual remains in contact, along with other individuals in relationships with these family members.

0   Significant family strengths. This level indicates a family with much love and mutual respect for each other. Family members are central in each other's lives.

1   Moderate level of family strengths. This level indicates a loving family with generally good communication and ability to enjoy each other's company. There may be some problems between family members.

2   Mild level of family strengths. Family is able to communicate and participate in each other's lives, however, family members may not be able to provide significant emotional or concrete support for each other.

3   This level indicates an individual with no known family strengths.

Interpersonal

This item is used to refer to the interpersonal skills of the individual as they relate to others.

0   Significant interpersonal strengths. The individual is seen as well liked by others and has significant ability to form and maintain positive relationships. The individual has multiple close friends and is friendly with others.

1   Moderate level of interpersonal strengths. The individual has formed positive interpersonal relationships with peers and other non-caregivers. The individual may currently have no friends, but has a history of making and maintaining friendships with others.

2   Mild level of interpersonal strengths. The individual has some social skills that facilitate positive relationships with peers but may not have any current healthy relationships, but has a history of making and maintaining healthy friendships with others.

3   This level indicates an individual with no known interpersonal strengths. The individual currently does not have any friends nor has he/she had any friends in the past.

Relationship Permanence

This item refers to the stability of significant relationships in the individual's life, likely including family members but also others (do not include paid relationships such as service providers).

0   This level indicates an individual who has very stable relationships. Family members, friends, and community have been stable for most of his/her life and are likely to remain so in the foreseeable future.

1   This level indicates an individual who has had stable relationships but there is some concern about instability in the near future (one year) due to transitions or illness.

2   This level indicates an individual who has had at least one stable relationship over his/her lifetime but has experienced other instability through factors such as divorce, moving, removal from the home, and death.

3   This level indicates an individual who does not have any stability in relationships.

Educational/Vocational

This item is used to refer to the strengths of the school/vocational environment and may or may not reflect any specific educational/work skills possessed by the individual.

0   This level indicates an individual who is in school or employed and is involved with an educational plan or work environment that appears to exceed expectations. There is no potential for job loss or the school works exceptionally well with the individual and family to create a special learning environment.

1   This level indicates an individual who is working or in school, however, there have been problems such as tardiness, absenteeism, reductions in productivity, or conflict with supervisors or teachers.

2   This level indicates an individual who is either in school but has a plan that does not appear to be effective or is temporary unemployed. A history of consistent employment should be demonstrated and the potential for future employment without the need for vocational rehabilitation should be evidenced. This also may indicate an individual with a clear vocational preference.

3   This level indicates an individual who has dropped out of school or is in a school setting that does not further his/her education. This level also indicates significant vocational impairment. This may be characterized by either chronic unemployment, as defined by at least three years without consistent employment, or evidence that vocational rehabilitation would be necessary in order to be employed in a competitive work environment. This level indicates an individual with no known or identifiable vocational skill and no expression of any future vocational preferences.

Well-Being

This rating should be based on the psychological strength that the individual may have developed including both the ability to enjoy positive life experiences and manage negative life experiences. This should be rated independent to the individual's current level of distress.

0   This level indicates an individual with exceptional psychological strengths. Both coping and savoring skills are well developed.

1   This level indicates an individual with good psychological strengths. The person has solid coping skills for managing distress or solid savoring skills for enjoying pleasurable events.

2   This level indicates an individual with limited psychological strengths. For example, a person with very low self-esteem would be rated here.

3   This level indicates an individual with no known or identifiable psychological strengths. This may be due to intellectual impairment or serious psychiatric disorders.

Spiritual/Religious

This rating should be based on the individual's involvement in spiritual or religious beliefs and activities.

0   This level indicates an individual with strong religious and spiritual strengths. The individual may be very involved in a religious community or may have strongly held spiritual or religious beliefs that can sustain or comfort him/her in difficult times.

1   This level indicates an individual with some religious and spiritual strengths. The individual may be involved in a religious community.

2   This level indicates an individual with few spiritual or religious strengths. The individual may have little contact with religious institutions.

3   This level indicates an individual with no known spiritual or religious involvement.

Talents/Interests

This rating should be based broadly on any talent, creative or artistic skills an individual may have including art, theater, music, athletics, and so forth.

0   This level indicates an individual with significant creative/artistic strengths. An individual who receives a significant amount of personal benefit from activities surrounding a talent would be rated here.

1   This level indicates an individual with a notable talent. Fore example, an individual who is involved in athletics or plays a musical instrument would be rated here.

2   This level indicates an individual who has expressed interest in developing a specific talent or talents even if they have not developed that talent to date.

3   This level indicates an individual with no known talents, interests or hobbies.

Inclusion

This rating should be based on the individual's level of involvement in the cultural aspects of life in his/her community.

0   This level indicates an individual with extensive and substantial long-term ties with the community. For example, involvement in a community group for more than one year, may be widely accepted by neighbors, or involved in other community activities or informal networks.

1   This level indicates an individual with significant community ties although they may be relatively short-term (i.e., past year).

2   This level indicates an individual with limited ties and/or supports from the community.

3   This level indicates an individual with no known ties or supports from the community.

References

American Law Institute. (1962). *Model penal code.* Proposed official draft. Philadelphia.

Anderson, R. L., & Lyons, J. S. (2001). Needs-based planning for persons with serious mental illness residing in intermediate care facilities. *Journal of Behavioral Health Services Research,* 28(1), 104-110.

Andrews, D. A., & Bonta, J. (1994). *The psychology of criminal conduct.* Cincinnati, OH: Anderson Publishing Co.

Andoh, B. (1993). The M'Naghten rules—the story so far. *Medico-Legal Journal,* 61(1), 93-103.

Appelbaum, P. S., Robbins, P. C., & Monahan, J. (2000). Violence and delusions: Data from the MacArthur Violence Risk Assessment Study. *American Journal of Psychiatry,* 157, 566-572.

Arboleda-Florez, J. (1998). Mental illness and violence: An epidemiological appraisal of the evidence. *Canadian Journal of Psychiatry,* 43(10), 989-996.

Arboleda-Florez, J., Holley, H., & Crisanti, A. (1998). Mental illness and violence. *International Medical Journal,* 5(1), 3-8.

Arseneault, L., Moffitt, T. E., Caspi, A., & Taylor, P. J. (2000). Mental disorders and violence in a total birth cohort: Results from the Dunedin study. *Archives of General Psychiatry,* 57, 979-986.

Baxstrom v. Herold, 383 U.S. 107 (1966).

Belkin, J., Blumstein, A., & Glass, W. (1973). Recidivism as a feedback process: An analytical model and empirical validation. *Journal of Criminal Justice,* 1, 7-26.

Bellak, A., & Gearon, J. (2002). Substance abuse treatment for people with schizophrenia. *Addictive Behaviors,* 23(6), 749-766.

Berman, M., & Coccaro, E. F. (1998). Neurobiological correlates of violence: Relevance to criminal responsibility. *Behavioral Sciences and the Law,* 16, 303-318.

Bieber, S. L., Pasewark, R. A., Bosten, K., & Steadman, H. J. (1988). Predicting criminal recidivism of insanity acquittees. *International Journal of Law and Psychiatry,* 11, 105-112.

181

Bigelow, D. A., Bloom, J. D., & Williams, M. (1990). Costs of managing insanity acquittees under a psychiatric security review board system. *Hospital and Community Psychiatry*, 41(6), 613-614.

Bigelow, D. A., Bloom, J. D., Williams, M., & McFarland, B. H. (1999). An administrative model for close monitoring and managing high risk individuals. *Behavioral Sciences and the Law*, 17, 227-235.

Blau, G. L., & Pasewark, R. A. (1994). Satutory changes and the insanity defense: Seeking the perfect insane person. *Law and Psychology Review*, 18, 69.

Bloom, J. D., Rogers, J. L., Manson, S. M., & Williams, M. H. (1986). Lifetime police contacts of discharged psychiatric security review board clients. *International Journal of Law and Psychiatry*, 8, 189-202.

Bloom, J. D., & Williams, M. H. (1994). *Management and treatment of insanity Acquittees: A model for the 1990s*. Washington D.C.: American Psychiatric Press.

Bloom, J. D., Williams, M. H., & Bigelow, D. A. (1991). Monitored conditional release of persons found not guilty by reason of insanity. *American Journal of Psychiatry*, 148, 444-448.

Bloom, J. D., Williams, M. H., Rogers, J. L., & Barbur, P. (1986). Evaluation and treatment of insanity acquittees in the community. *Bulletin of the American Academy of Psychiatry and Law*, 14(3), 231-244.

Boehnert, C. E. (1987). Characteristics of those evaluated for insanity. *Journal of Psychiatry & Law*, 15(2), 229-246.

Boehnert, C. E. (1985). Psychological and demographic factors associated with individuals using the insanity defense. *Journal of Psychiatry & Law*, 13(1-2), 9-31.

Bogenberger, R. P., Pasewark, R. A., Gudeman, H., & Beiber, S. L. (1987). Follow-up of insanity acquittees in Hawaii. *International Journal of Law and Psychiatry*, 10, 283-295.

Boman, B. (1990). Are all Vietnam veterans like John Rambo? *American Psychiatric Press*, 16, 270.

Bonta, J., Hanson, K., & Law, M. (1998). The prediction of criminal and violent recidivism among mentally disordered offenders: A meta-analysis. *Psychological Bulletin*. 123(2), 123-142.

Borum, R., & Fulero, S. M. (1999). Empirical research on the insanity defense and attempted reforms: Evidence toward informed policy. *Law and Human Behavior*, 23(1), 1999.

Brown, K. (2003). *Presentation to the 2003 NASMHPD Meeting*, Little Rock, Arkansas.

Callahan, L. A., Mayer, C., & Steadman, H. J. (1987). Post-Hinckley Insanity Defense Reforms in the United States. *Mental and Physical Disability Law Reporter, 11(1), 54-59.*

Callahan, L. A., & Silver, E. (1998). Factors associated with the conditional release of persons acquitted by reason of insanity: A decision tree approach. *Law and Human Behavior*, 22(2), 147-163.

Carroll, A., Lyall, M., & Forrester, A. (2004). Clinical hopes and public fears in forensic mental health. *Journal of Forensic Psychiatry and Psychology*, 15(3), 407-425.

Cavanaugh, J. L., & Wasyliw, O. E. (1985). Treating the not guilty by reason of insanity outpatient: A two-year study. *Bulletin of the American Academy of Psychiatry and Law*, 13(4), 407-415.

Chou, K., Liu, S., & Chu, H. (2002). The effects of support groups on caregivers of patients with schizophrenia. *International Journal of Nursing Studies*, 39(7), 713-722.

Cirincione, C., & Jacobs, C. (1999). Identifying insanity acquittals: Is it any easier? *Law and Human Behavior*, 23(4), 487-497.

Cirincione, C., Steadman, H. J., & McGreevy, M. A. (1995). Rates of insanity acquittals and the factors associated with successful insanity pleas. *Bulletin of the American Academy of Psychiatry and Law*, 23(3), 399-409.

Clark, C. R., Holden, C. E., Thompson, J. S., Watson, P. L., & Wightman, L. H. (1993). Forensic treatment in the United States: A survey of selected forensic hospitals. Treatment at Michigan's Forensic Center. *International Journal of Law and Psychiatry*, 16(1-2), 71-81.

Crisp, A., Gelder, M., Rix, S., & Meltzer, H. (2000). Stigmatisation of people with mental illnesses. *British Journal of Psychiatry*, 177, 4-7.

Ditton P.M. (1999). Mental Health Treatment of Inmates and Probationers. Washington, DC, US Department of Justice.

Di Masso, J., Avi-Itzhak, T., & Obler, D. R. (2001). The clubhouse model: An outcome study on attendance, work attainment and status, and hospitalization recidivism. *Work*, 17(1), 23-30.

Diestelhorst, S., Koller, M., & Mueller, P. (2001). Frequency and length of stay in in-patient treatment of schizophrenia patients in two psychiatric hospitals: A study over two decades. *Psychiatric Illness*, 12(3), 99-104.

Douglas, K. S., Ogloff, J. R., Nicholls, T. L., & Grant, I. (1999). Assessing risk for violence among psychiatric patients: The HCR-20 violence risk assessment scheme and the psychopathy checklist: Screening version. *Journal of Consulting Psychology*, 67(6), 917-930.

Dvoskin, J. A., & Spiers, E. M. (2004). On the role of correctional officers in prison mental health. *Psychiatric Quarterly*, 75(1), 41-59.

Elbogen, E. B., & Tomkins, A. J. (2000). From the psychiatric hospital to the community: Integrating conditional release and contingency management. *Behavioral Sciences and the Law*, 18, 427-444.

Eronen, M., Hakola, P., & Tiihonen, J. (1996). Factors associated with homicide recidivism in a 13-year sample of homicide offenders in Finland, *Psychiatric Services*, 47, 403-406.

Farabee, D., Shen, H., & Sanchez, S. (2002). Perceived coercion and treatment need among mentally ill parolees. *Criminal Justice and Behavior*, 29(1), 76-86.

Fontana, A., Schwartz, L. S., & Rosenheck, R. (1997). Posttraumatic Stress Disorder among female Vietnam veterans: A causal model of etiology. *American Journal of Public Health*, 87(2), 169-175.

Friedman, S. H., Hrouda, D. R., Holden, C. E., Noffsinger, S. G., & Resnick, P. J. (2005). Child murder committed by severely mentally ill mothers: An examination of mothers found not guilty by reason of insanity. *Journal of Forensic Science*, 50(6), 1-6.

Friedman, M. J., & Schnurr, P. P. (1995). The relationship between trauma, post-traumatic stress disorder, and physical health. In M. J. Friedman, D. S. Charney, and A. Y. Deutch (Eds.), *Neurobiological and clinical consequences of stress: From normal adaption to PTSD (pp. 507-524)*. Philadelphia: Lippincott-Raven.

Fukanaga, K. K., Pasewark, R. A., Hawkins, M., & Gudeman, H. (1981). Insanity plea: Interexaminer agreement and concordance of psychiatric opinion and court verdict. *Law and Human Behavior*, 5(4), 325-328.

Gardner, W., Lidz, C. W., Mulvey, E. P., & Shaw E. C. (1996). Clinical versus actuarial predictions of violence in patients with mental illnesses. *Journal of Consulting and Clinical Psychology*, 64(3), 602-609.

Gendreau, P., Little, T., & Goggin, C. (1996). A meta-analysis of the predictors of adult offender recidivism: What works. *Criminology*, 34, 575-607.

Goethe, J., Dornelas, E., & Fischer, E. (1996). A cluster analytic study of functional outcome after psychiatric hospitalization. *Comprehensive Psychiatry*, 37(2), 115-121.

Goldmeier, J., Sauer, R. H., & White, V. (1977). A halfway house for mentally ill offenders. *American Journal of Psychiatry*, 134(1), 45-49.

Goldmeier, J., White, E. V., Ulrich, C., & Klein, G. A. (1980). Community intervention with the mentally ill offender. *Bulletin of American Academy of Psychiatry and Law*, 8, 72-81.

Gottfredson, M. R., & Hirschi, T. (1990). *A general theory of crime*. Stanford: Stanford University Press.

Grafman, J., Schwab, K., Warden, D., Pridgen, A., Brown, H. R., & Salazar, A. M. (1996). Frontal lobe injuries, violence, and aggression: A report of the Vietnam Head Injury Study. *Neurology*, 46, 1231-1738.

Greene, G. J., Lee, M, Trask, R., & Rheinscheld, J. (2005). How to word with clients' strengths in crisis intervention: A solution-focused approach. In A. Roberts (Ed.), *Crisis intervention handbook: Assessment, treatment, and research*, 3rd ed. (pp. 64-89). New York: Oxford University Press.

Grella, C., & Gilmore, J. (2002). Improving service delivery to the dually diagnosed in Los Angeles County. *Journal of Substance Abuse Treatment*, 23(2), 115-122.

Grisso, T., Davis, J., Vesselinov, R., Appelbaum, P. S., & Monohan, J. (2000). Violent thoughts and violent behavior following hospitalization for mental disorder. *Journal of Consulting and Clinical Psychology*, 68(3), 388-398.

Gutheil, T. G. (1999). A confusion of tongues: Competence, insanity, psychiatry, and the law. *Psychiatry Services*, 50(6), 767-773.

Eronen, R., Hakola, P., & Tiihonen, J. (1996). Mental disorders and homicidal behavior in Finland. *Archives of General Psychiatry*, 53(6), 497-501.

Feder, L. (1991). A comparison of the community adjustment of mentally ill offenders with those from the general prison population: An 18-month follow-up. *Law and Human Behavior*, 15(5), 477-493.

Friedman, S. H., Hrouda, D. R., Holden, C. E., Noffsinger, S. G., & Resnick, P. J. (2005). Child murder committed by severely mentally ill mothers: An examination of mothers found not guilty by reason of insanity. *Journal of Forensic Science*, 50(6), 1466-71.

Haggard-Grann, U. & Gumpert, C. (2005). The violence relapse process – a qualitative analysis of high-risk situations and risk communication in mentally disordered offenders. *Psychology, Crime & Law*, 11(2), 199-222.

Hans, V. P., & Slater, D. (1983). John Hinckley, Jr. and the insanity defense: The public's verdict. *Public Opinion Quarterly*, 47(2), 202-212.

Harris, V. L. (2000). Insanity acquittees and rearrest: The past 24 years. *Journal of American Academy of Psychiatry and Law*, 28, 225-231.

Harris, V., & Koepsell, T. D. (1996). Criminal recidivism in mentally ill offenders: A pilot study. Bulletin of the American Academy of Psychiatry and Law, 24(2), 177-186.

Harris, V., & Koepsell, T. D. (1998). Rearrest among mentally ill offenders. *Journal of the American Academy of Psychiatry and Law*, 26(3), 393-402.

Heilburn, K., & Griffin, P. A. (1993). Community-based forensic treatment of insanity acquittees. *International Journal of Law and Psychiatry*, 16, 133-150.

Heilbrun, K., Lawson, K., Spier, S., & Libby, J. (1994). Community placement for insanity acquittees: A preliminary study of residential programs and person-situation fit. *Bulletin of the American Academy of Psychiatry and Law*, 22(4), 551-560.

Higgins, S. A. (1991). Post-traumatic stress disorder and its role in the defense of Vietnam veterans. *Law & Psychology Review*, 15, 259-276.

Hodgins, S., Hiscoke, U. L., & Freese, R. (2003). The antecedents of aggressive behavior among men with Schizophrenia: A prospective investigation of patients in community treatment. *Behavioral Sciences and the Law*, 21, 523-546.

Hodgins, S. & Mueller-Isberner, R. (2004). Preventing crime by people with schizophrenic disorders: The role of psychiatric services. *British Journal of Psychiatry*, 185, 245-250.

Hodgins, S., Mednick, S. A., Brennan, P. A., Schulsinger, F., & Engberg, M. (1996). Mental disorder and crime: Evidence from a Danish birth cohort. *Archives of General Psychiatry*, 53(6), 489-496.

Hooper, J. F., McLearen, A. M., & Barnett, M. E. (2005). The Alabama Structured Assessment of Treatment Completion for Insanity Acquittes (The AlaSATcom). *International Journal of Law and Psychiatry*, 28(6), 604-612.

Jacobi, J. V. (2005). Prison health, public health: Obligations and opportunities. *American Journal of Law and Medicine*, 31, 447-478.

Janofsky, J. S., Dunn, M. H., Roskes, E. J., Briskin, J. K., & Rudolph, M. L. (1996). Insanity defense pleas in Baltimore City: An analysis of outcome. *American Journal of Psychiatry*, 153, 1464-1468.

Jemelka, R. P., Trupin, E., & Chiles, J. A. The mentally ill in prison: A review. *Hospital and Community Psychiatry*, 40, 481-491.

Johnson, D. R., Rosenheck, R., Fontana, A., Lubin, H., Charney, D., & Southwick, S. (1996). Outcome of intensive inpatient treatment for combat-related posttraumatic stress disorder. *American Journal of Psychiatry*, 153, 771-777.

Kessler, R. C., Sonnega, A., Bromet, E., Hughes, M., & Nelson, C. (1995). Posttraumatic Stress Disorder in the National Comorbidity Survey. *Archives of General Psychiatry*, 52(12), 1048-1060.

Kravitz, H. M., & Kelly, J. (1999). An outpatient psychiatry program for offenders with mental disorders found not guilty by reason of insanity. *Psychiatric Services*, 50(12), 1597-1605.

Kubiak, S. P. (2004). The effects of PTSD on treatment adherence, drug relapse, and criminal recidivism in a sample of incarcerated men and women. *Research on Social Work Practice*, 14(6), 424-433.

Kulka R. A., Schlenger W. E., Fairbank J.A., Hough R.L., Jordan B. K., Marmar C. R., Weiss D.S. (1990). *Trauma and the Vietnam war generation: Report of findings from the national Vietnam veterans readjustment study*. New York: Brunner/Mazel.

Lamb, H. R., Weinberger, L. E., & Gross, B. H. (1988). Court-mandated community outpatient treatment for persons found not guilty by reason of insanity: A five-year follow-up. *American Journal of Psychiatry*, 145(4), 450-456.

Lamb, H. R., Weinberger, L. E., & Gross, B. H. (1989). Court-mandated outpatient treatment for insanity acquittees: Clinical philosophy and implementation. *Hospital and Community Psychiatry*, 39(10), 1080-1084.

Lande, R. G. (1990). Disposition of insanity acquittees in the United States military. *Bulletin of American Psychiatry & Law*, 18(3), 303-309.

Lande, R. G. (1991). The military insanity defense. *Bulletin of American Psychiatry and Law*, 19(2), 193-201.

Lawrie, S. M. (1999). Stigmatization of psychiatric disorder. *Psychiatric Bulletin*, 23(3), 129-131.

Lindquist, P., & Allebeck, P. (1990). Schizophrenia and crime: A longitudinal follow-up of 644 schizophrenics in Stockholm. *British Journal of Psychiatry*, 157, 345-350.

Linhorst, D. M. (1999). The unconditional release of mentally ill offenders from indefinite commitment: A study of Missouri insanity acquittees. *Journal of the American Academy of Psychiatry and Law*, 27(4), 563-579.

Linhorst, D. M., Hunsucker, L., & Parker, L. D. (1998). An examination of gender and racial differences among Missouri insanity acquittees. *Journal of the American Academy of Psychiatry and the Law*, 26(3), 411-424.

Link, B. G., Andrews, H., & Cullen, F. T. (1992). The violent and illegal behavior of mental patients reconsidered. *American Sociological Review*, 57, 275-292.

Link, B., & Stueve, A. (1994). Psychotic symptoms and the violent/illegal behavior of mental patients compared to community controls. In J. Monahan & H. Steadman (Eds.), *Violence and mental disorder: Developments in risk assessment* (pp.137-159). Chicago: University of Chicago Press.

Liu, H. (1997). Burnout and organizational commitment among staff of publicly funded substance abuse treatment programs. *Dissertation Abstracts*, 58(6A), 2386.

Luettgen, J., Chrapko, W. E., & Reddon, J. R. (1998). Preventing violent re-offending in not criminally responsible patients. *International Journal of Law and Psychiatry*, 21(1), 89-98.

Lymburner, J. A., & Roesch, R. (1999). The insanity defense: Five years of research, 1993-1997. (1999). *International Journal of Psychiatry and Law*, 22(3-4), 213-240.

Lyons, J. S., Colletta, J., Devens, M., & Finkel, S.I. (1995). The validity of the Severity of Psychiatric Illness in a sample of inpatients in a psychogeriatrics unit. *International Psychogeriatrics*, 7, 407-416.

Lyons, J. S., Stutesman, J., Neme, J., Vessey, J. T., O'Mahoney, M. T., & Camper, H. J. (1997). Predicting readmissions to the psychiatric emergency admissions and hospital outcomes. *Medical Care*, 35, 792-800.

MacAuley, F. (1993). *Insanity, Psychiatry and Criminal Responsibility*. Dublin: Round Hall Press.

Marciniak, R. D. (1986). Implications to forensic psychiatry of Post-Traumatic Stress Disorder: A review. *Military Medicine*, 151, 434-437.

Matthews, S. (2004). Failed agency and the insanity defense. *International Journal of Law and Psychiatry*, 27(5), 413-424.

Mayer A., & Barry, D. D. (1992). Working with the media to destigmatize mental illness. *Hospital and Community Psychiatry*, 43, 77-78.

McGreevy, M. A., Steadman, H. J., Dvoskin, J. A., & Dollard, N. (1991). New York State's system of managing insanity acquittees in the community. *Hospital and Community Psychiatry*, 42(5), 512-517.

Metzner, J. L. (2002). Prison litigation in the USA. The *Journal of Forensic Psychiatry*, 13(2), 240-244.

Miller, R. D. (2002). Automatic commitment of insanity acquittees: Keeping up with the *Jones*? *Journal of Psychiatry and Law*, 30, 59-95.

Monahan, J. (1992). Mental disorder and violent behavior: Perceptions and evidence. *American Psychologist*, 47, 511-521.

Monahan, J. (1993). Mental disorder and violence: Another look. In S. Hodgins (Ed.), *Mental disorder and crime* (pp.287-302). Newbury Park, CA: Sage.

Morgan, C. A., Hill, S., Fox, P., Kingham, P., & Southwick, M. (1999). Anniversary reactions in gulf war veterans: A follow-up inquiry 6 years after the war. *American Journal of Psychiatry*, 156, 1075-1079.

Morrall, P. (2000). *Madness and Murder*. London: Whurr.

Morrow, W. R., & Peterson, D. B. (1966). Follow-up of discharged psychiatric offenders: Not guilty by reason of insanity and criminal sexual psychopaths. *Journal of Criminal Law, Criminology and Police Science*, 57(1), 31-34.

Morse, S. J. (1999). Craziness and criminal responsibility. *Behavioral Sciences and the Law*, 17, 147-164.

Moscowitz, J. L., Lewis, R. J., Ito, M. S., & Ehrmentraut, J. (1999). MMPI-2 Profiles of NGRI and Civil Patients. *Journal of Clinical Psychology*, 55(5), 659-668.

National Mental Health Association (1983). *Myths and realities: A report of the National Commission on the Insanity Defense.* Arlington, VA: Author.

Nicholson, R. A., Norwood, S., & Enyart, C. (1991). Characteristics and outcomes of insanity acquittees in Oklahoma. *Behavioral Sciences and the Law*, 9, 487-500.

Norwood, S., Nicholson, R. A., Enyart, C., & Hickey, M. L. (1992). Insanity acquittal in Oklahoma: Recommendations for program planning and social policy. *Forensic Reports*, 5, 5-28.

Packer, I. K. (1983). Post-traumatic stress disorder and the insanity defense: A critical analysis. *Journal of Psychiatry and Law*, 11(2), 125-136.

Pantle, M. L., Pasewark, R. A., Steadman, H. J. (1981). Comparing institutionalization periods and subsequent arrests of insanity acquittees and convicted felons. *Journal of Psychiatry and Law*, 4, 305-316.

Pasewark, R. A. (1986). A review of research on the insanity defense. *Annals of the American Academy of Psychiatry and the Social Sciences*, 484, 100-115.

Pasewark, R. A., Pantle M. L., & Steadman, H. J. (1979). The insanity plea in New York State, 1965-1976. *New York State Bar Journal*, 186-225.

Pasewark, R. A., Pantle, M. L., & Steadman, H. J. (1982). Detention and rearrest rates of persons found not guilty by reason of insanity and convicted felons. *American Journal of Psychiatry*, 139(7), 892-897.

Pasewark, R. A., Seidenzahl, D., & Pantle, M. (1981). Opinions concerning criminality among mental patients. *Journal of Community Psychology*, 9(4), 367-370.

People v. Wood: Case No. 80-7410. Circuit Court of Cook County, Illinois, 1982.

Perlin, M. (1996). Myths, realities, and the political world: The anthropology of insanity defense attitudes. *Bulletin of the American Academy of Psychiatric Law*, 24(1), 5-26.

Petrila, J. (1982). The insanity defense and other mental health dispositions in Missouri. *International Journal of Law and Psychiatry*, 5(1), 81-101.

Phelan, L.C, & Link, B.G. (1998). The growing belief that people with mental illnesses are violent: The role of the dangerousness criterion for civil commitment. *Social Psychiatry & Psychiatric Epidemiology*, 33(1), S7-S12.

Phillips, B. L., & Pasewark, R. A. (1980). Insanity plea in Connecticut. *Bulletin of the American Academy of Psychiatry and Law*, 3(3), 335-344.

Phillips, H. K., Gray, N. S., MacCulloch, S. I., Taylor, J., Moore, S. C., Huckle, P., & MacCulloch, J. (2005). Risk assessment in offenders with mental disorders: Relative efficacy of personal demographic, criminal history, and clinical variables. *Journal of Interpersonal Violence*, 20(7), 833-847.

Pilisuk, M. (1975). The legacy of the Vietnam veteran. *Journal of Social Issues*, 31(4), 3-12.

Quinsey, V. L., Pruesse, M, &Fernley, R. (1975). A follow-up of patients found unfit to stand trial or not guilty because of insanity. *Journal of the Canadian Psychiatric Association*, 20, 461-467.

Randolph, R. L., & Pasewark, R. A. (1983). Characteristics, dispositions, and subsequent arrests of defendants pleading insanity in a rural state. *Journal of Psychiatry and Law*, 345-360.

Rice, M. (1997). Violent offender research and implications for the criminal justice system. *American Psychologist*, 52(4), 414-423.

Rice, M., & Harris, G. T. (1995). Violent recidivism: Assessing predictive validity. *Journal of Consulting and Clinical Psychology*, 63(5), 737-748.

Rice, M., Harris, G. T., Lang, C., & Bell, V. (1991). Recidivism among male insanity acquittees. *Journal of Psychiatry and Law*, 18, 379-403.

Rogers, J. L., & Bloom, J. D. (1982). Characteristics of persons committed to Oregon's psychiatric security review board. *Bulletin of the American Academy of Psychiatry and the Law*, 10(32), 155-164.

Rogers, J. L., Bloom, J. D., & Manson, S. M. (1984). Oregon's new insanity defense system: A review of the first five years, 1978 to 1982. *Bulletin of the American Academy of Psychiatry and the Law*, 12(4), 383-402.

Schanda, H., Knecht, G., Schreinzer, D., Stompe, Th., Ortwein-Swoboda, G., & Waldhoer, Th. (2004). Homicide and major mental disorders: A 25-year study. *Acta Psychiatrica Scandinavica*, 110, 98-107.

Schuerman, L. A., & Kobrin, S. (1984). Exposure of community mental health clients to the criminal justice system: Client/criminal or patient/prisoner. In L.A. Teplin (Ed.), *Mental health and criminal justice* (pp. 87-118). Beverly Hills, CA: Sage.

Scott, D. C., Zonana, H. V., & Getz, M. A. (1990). Monitoring insanity acquittees: Connecticut's psychiatric security review board. *Hospital and Community Psychiatry*, 41(9), 980-984.

Seig, A., Ball, E., & Menninger, L. A. (1995). A comparison of female versus male insanity aquittees in Colorado. *Bulletin of the American Academy of Psychiatry and the Law*, 23(4), 523-532.

Sellwood, W., Barrowclough, C., Tarrier, N., Quinn, J., Mainwaring, J., & Lewis, S. (2002). Needs-based cognitive-behavioral family intervention for carers of patients suffering from schizophrenia: 12 month follow-up. *Acta Psychiatrica Scandinavica*, 104(5), 346-355.

Shah, S. (1990). The mentally disordered offenders: Some issues of policy and planning. In E.H. Cox-Feith, & B.N.W. de Smit (Eds.), *Innovations in mental health legislation and government policy: A European perspective*. The Hague: The Netherlands Ministry of Justice.

Silver, E. (1995). Punishment or treatment? Comparing the lengths of confinement of successful and unsuccessful insanity defendants. *Law and Human Behavior*, 19(4), 375-388.

Silver, E., Mulvey, E. P., & Monohan, J. (1999). Assessing violence risk among discharged psychiatric patients: Toward an ecological approach. *Law and Human Behavior*, 23(2), 237-255.

Silver, S. B., Cohen, M. I., & Spodak, M. K. (1989). Follow-up after release of insanity acquittees, mentally disordered offenders, and convicted felons. *Bulletin of the American Academy of Psychiatry and the Law*, 17(4), 387-400.

Silverberg, J., Vital, T., & Brakel, S. (2001). Breaking down barriers to mandated outpatient treatment for mentally ill offenders. *Psychiatric Annals*, 31(7), 433-440.

Singer, J. D., & Willett, J. B. (1991). Modeling the days of our lives: Using survival analysis when designing and analyzing longitudinal studies of duration and the timing of events. *Psychological Bulletin*, 110(2), 268-290.

Slobogin, C. (2003). The integrationist alternative to the insanity defense: Reflections on the exculpatory scope of mental illness in the wake of the Andrea Yates trial. *American Journal of Criminal Law*, 30(3), 315-341.

Slovenko, R. (2004). The watering down of PTSD in criminal law. Journal of Psychiatry & Law, 32, 411-438.

Sosowsky, L. (1980). Explaining the increased arrest rate among mental patients: A cautionary note. *American Journal of Psychiatry*, 137, 1602-1605.

Sparr, L. F., & Atkinson, R. M. (1986). Posttraumatic stress disorder as an insanity defense: Medicolegal quicksand. *American Journal of Psychiatry*, 143(5), 608-613.

Spodak, M. K., Silver, S. B., & Wright, C. U. (1984). Criminality of discharged insanity acquittees: Fifteen year experience in Maryland reviewed. *Bulletin of the American Academy of Psychiatry and* Law, 12(4), 373-383.

Sreenivasan, S., Kirkish, P., Shoptaw, S., Welsh, R. K., & Ling, W. (2000). Neuropsychological and diagnostic differences between recidivistically violent not criminally responsible and mentally ill prisoners. *International Journal of Law and Psychiatry*, 23(2), 161-172.

Stafford, K. P., & Karpawich, J. J. (1997). Conditional Release: Court-ordered outpatient treatment for insanity acquittees. *New Directions for Mental* Health Services, 75, 61-72.

Steadman, H. J. (1980). Insanity acquittals in New York State, 1965-1978. *American Journal of Psychiatry*, 137(3), 321-326.

Steadman, H. J. (1985). Empirical research on the insanity defense. *Annals of the American Academy of Psychiatry and the Social Sciences*, 477, 58-71.

Steadman, H., & Cocozza, J. (1978). Selective reporting and the public's misconceptions of the criminally insane. *Public Opinion Quarterly*, 41, 523-533.

Steadman, H. J., Cocozza, J. J., & Melick, M. E. (1978). Explaining the increased arrest rate among mental patients: The changing clientele of state hospitals. *American Journal of Psychiatry*, 135, 816-820.

Steadman, H. J., & Keveles, G. (1972). The community adjustment and criminal activity of the Baxstrom patients: 1966-1970. *American Journal of Psychiatry*, 129(3), 80-86.

Steadman, H. J., McGreevy, M. A., Morrissey, J. P., Callahan, L. A., Robbins, P. C., & Cirincione, C. (1993). *Before and after Hinckley: Evaluating insanity defense reform*. New York: Guilford.

Steadman, H. J., Morris, S. M., & Dennis, D. L. (1995). The diversion of mentally ill persons from jails to community-based services: A profile of programs. *American Journal of Public Health*, 85, 1630-1635.

Steadman, H. J., & Ribner, S. A. (1980). Changing perceptions of the mental health needs of inmates in local jail. *American Journal of Psychiatry*, 137, 1115-1116.

Swanson, L.W. (1994). Mental disorder, substance abuse, and community violence: An epidemiological approach. In L. Monahan & H. Steadman (Eds.), *Violence and mental disorder: Developments in risk assessment* (pp. 101-136). Chicago: University of Chicago Press.

Swanson, J. W., Borum, R., Swartz, M. S., Monahan, J. (1996). Psychotic symptoms and disorders and the risk of violent behavior in the community. *Criminal Behaviour & Mental Health,* 6(4), 309-329.

Swanson, J. W., Holzer, C. E., Ganju, V. K., & Jono, R. T. (1990). Violence and psychiatric disorder in the community: Evidence from the Epidemiologic Catchment Area surveys. *Hospital and Community Psychiatry*, 41, 761-770.

Teplin, L. A. (1985). The criminality of the mentally ill: A dangerous misconception. *American Journal of Psychiatry*, 142, 593-599.

Teplin, L. A. (1990). The prevalence of severe mental disorder among male urban jail detainees: Comparison with the Epidemiologic Catchment Area program. *American Journal of Public Health*, 84, 290-293.

Teplin, L. A., Abram, K. M., & McClelland, G. M. (1994). Does psychiatric disorder predict violent crime among released jail detainees? *American Psychologist*, 49(4), 335-342.

Timko, C., & Moos, R. (2002). Symptom severity, amount of treatment and 1-year outcomes among dual diagnosis patients. *Administration and Policy in Mental Health*, 30(1), 35-54.

United States Department of Justice: Prison and jail inmates at midyear 2002. *Bureau of Justice Statistics*, NJC 198877, April 2003.

Vartianinen, H., & Hakola, P. (1992). Monitored conditional release of persons found not guilty by reason of insanity. *American Journal of Psychiatry*, 149(3), 415.

Wahl. O. F. (1992). Mass media images of mental illness: A review of the literature. *Journal of Community Psychology*, 20, 343-352.

Walker, E. (2000). Spiritual support in relation to community violence exposure, aggressive outcomes, and psychological adjustment among inner-city young adolescents. *Dissertation Abstracts*, 61(6B), 3295.

Walko, S., Pratt, C., Siiter, R., & Ellison, K. (1993). Predicting staff retention in psychiatric rehabilitation. *Psychosocial Rehabilitation Journal*, 16(3), 150-153.

Walsh, E., Buchanan, A., & Fahy, T. (2002). Violence and schizophrenia: Examining the evidence. *British Journal of Psychiatry*, 180, 490-495.

Watson, A., Hanrahan, P, Luchins, D., & Lurigio, A. (2001). Mental health courts and the complex issue of mentally ill offenders. *Psychiatric Services*, 52, 477-481.

Weideranders, M. R. (1992). Recidivism of disordered offenders who were conditionally vs. unconditionally released. *Behavioral Sciences and the Law*, 10, 141-148.

Wiederanders, M. R., Bromley, D. L., & Choate, P. A. (1997). Forensic conditional release programs and outcomes in three states. *International Journal of Law and Psychiatry*, 20(2), 249-257.

Wiederanders, M. R., & Choate, P. A. (1994). Beyond recidivism: Measuring community adjustments of conditionally released insanity acquittees. *Psychological Assessment*, 6(1), 61-66.

Willett, J. B. & Singer, J. D. (1991). How long did it take? Using survival analysis in educational and psychological research. In L. M. Collins & J. L. Horn (Eds), *Best methods for the analysis of change: Recent advances, unanswered questions, future directions (pp. 310-327)*. Washington, DC: American Psychological Association.

Yesavage, J. A., Benezech, M., Larrieu-Arguille, R., Bourgeois, M, Tanke, E., Rager, P., et al. (1986). Recidivism of the criminally insane in France: A 22 year follow-up. *International Journal of Clinical Psychiatry*, 47(9), 465-466.

Zatzick, D. F., Maramar, C. R., Weiss, D. S., Browner, W. S., Metzler, T. J., Golding, J. M., et al.(1997). Posttraumatic Stress Disorder and functioning and quality of life outcomes in a nationally representative sample of male Vietnam veterans. *American Journal of Psychiatry*, 154(12), 1690-1695.

Zeidler, J. C., Haines, W. H., Tikuisis, V., & Uffelman, E. J. (1955). A follow-up study of patients discharged from a hospital for the criminally insane. *Journal of Social Therapy*, 1(2), 21-24.

Zonana, H. V., Bartel, R. L., Wells, J. A., Buchanan, J. A., & Getz, M. A. (1990). Part II: Sex differences in persons found not guilty by reason of insanity: Analysis of data from the Connecticut NGRI registry. *Bulletin of the American Academy of Psychiatry and the Law*, 18(2), 129-142.

Zonana, H. V., Wells, J. A., Getz, M. A., & Buchanan, J. A. (1990). The NGRI registry: Initial analyses of data collected on Connecticut insanity acquittees: I. *Bulletin of the American Academy of Psychiatry & the Law*, 18(2), 115-128.

Index